# SEX:
# THE RADICAL VIEW
# OF A CATHOLIC THEOLOGIAN

# SEX:
# THE RADICAL VIEW
# OF A CATHOLIC THEOLOGIAN

by

Michael F. Valente

THE BRUCE PUBLISHING COMPANY, NEW YORK

COLLIER-MACMILLAN LIMITED, LONDON

Library of Congress Catalog Card Number: 79-132466

The Bruce Publishing Company, New York
Collier-Macmillan Canada, Ltd., Toronto, Ontario

Made in the United States of America

To those who have given me
love, learning, and life.

# PREFACE

Modern religion has been justly criticized for its failure to take the lead in creating truly human, worthy, and sensitive guidelines for human conduct. It has been called imitative rather than original. Traditional theology has been accused of failing to deal with man's ever-expanding knowledge of himself and his world, and of not evolving in an integrated growth with man's scientific knowledge. It has been blamed for reacting rather than creating.

Yet, if theology is not to be a set of stagnant dogmatisms handed out under and excused by the title "orthodoxy," if it is not merely going to put its rubber stamp of approval on what it sees it cannot overcome, then it must be prepared to meet the challenge of mankind's rapid development. If, as man's rational knowledge increases, theology is to be an evolving attempt to articulate in an even clearer way man's faith commitment, then it must stand ready to deal with moral questions in the light of this new knowledge. This, in part, is its proper task.

One of the faults of the old theology was that it was academic and perfect to the point of often being irrelevant. Experience with that kind of theology has taught us that theology must leave the hallowed halls of academe and begin to develop new models based upon real experience. Evolutionary man is in a transitional phase in the history of his development. His present quest is for the freedom, and hence the power, to adopt a new world view. In a primary sense, this book is about freedom—freedom from the past and freedom for the future.

It is about freedom from the past because men of the past saw "the natural" as a static law within which man had to conduct his life. That attitude stemmed from a life-style and world view based on a broad consensus that there is an orthodox way of life; a specific, meaningful way providing the only true self-understanding; a way of life identified with the true way, one's country's way, God's way.

It is about freedom from the reactionary view of the unfree who see the liberated individual as a tremendous threat. To them, the truly free individual is like a murderer (a taker of life, purpose, and meaning) or a heretic (a threat to the sacredness of existence itself); he must be hung from the gallows or burned at the stake.

It is about freedom from feeling threatened by long-haired boys or lesbians because one is imprisoned by a world view that imputes sacredness—and hence gives sanction—only to a fixed order of things. For sacredness in this sense is what men read into that which they rely upon to give purpose to an otherwise meaningless existence. It is also about freedom from subconscious envy of those who are truly free, envy fired by the dread that acceptance of a changed world order would give credence to the possibility that one has missed out on the true meaning of life.

It is thus about freedom from the burden of a static world view, as well as freedom for change *to* another world view. And it is more. It is about freedom for recognition of and creative participation in the fact of man's evolution, an evolution which man himself—because he is rational and free—can direct.

Morality is the exclusive property of man because of his rationality. His ability to reflect upon his motives is the source of all morality, all restraint upon impulses to evil. Thus an act is moral (morally good *or* evil) insofar as it is the act of an agent who can be critical of himself and his behavior. Acts apart from the agent's reflection are neither moral nor immoral.

This kind of understanding of morality poses more questions than it answers, as will any attempt to seek the truth at any cost. It is usually easier to criticize than to suggest solutions. But such self-criticism is at least a first step toward illuminating a new direction.

It is written of Jesus that he said he is the Truth. In all that the Christian is and does he attempts to come closer to truth. This search for Jesus as the Truth is his religious quest. It is an intellectual quest which he must pursue relentlessly. The Christian must not fear either truth or life. He dare not shrink from facts but should welcome the opportunity to deal with reality: to rejoice with gratitude in what is good; to try to change what is evil; to take what is neither morally good nor evil and to try to transform it with love into what is clearly good.

This book stems from an interest in the history and form of innovatory thought in matters of sexual ethics. It is intended to be a contribution to the discussion of how and to what extent sexual acts can be judged, morally speaking, to be good or evil. It is above all intended to offer a new psychic orientation toward the role of sexuality in human life as a help to such judgment.

Michael F. Valente
New York City

# CONTENTS

# SEX:
# THE RADICAL VIEW
# OF A CATHOLIC THEOLOGIAN

# 1
# A PLEA
# FOR LIFE

God is a mystery, yet some men say that they know his ways. They attribute to him motivations which they claim they can understand and explain to others—for instance, they suggest that the reason why both pleasure and procreation are inherent in the sexual act is that God "in his infinite wisdom" added pleasure to the act (which is seen as an act of procreation) in order to induce men to engage in it. They never suggest that he might have made the act for man's pleasure and then, because he reasoned that man would indulge in it frequently, wisely attached the effect of procreation. Yet the latter suggestion seems as reasonable, if as arbitrary and anthropomorphic, as the former. It is time to pull back from facile attempts to assess divine motivation. It is time to move away from the view that human powers are limited to one specific purpose and no other. It is time for a change of viewpoint.

This book is about change, about a world and a Church in flux. It is about a theological problem, specifically about how some have exploited the guilt feelings of others in order to impose upon them social and economic restrictions. They have accomplished this by setting up standards for individual sexual behavior that they consider essential for perpetuating the present social structure and the world view which sees that structure as essentially static, fixed, and given as it were by nature, God, or simply those forces which transcend human control.

The book is also about the historical development of religious men's interpretations of Christianity's demands concerning sex, and the rule of human sexual ethics that became normative within Roman Catholicism. That rule, so rigid as to be thought irreformable, was challenged by the reality of a technological world in which contraception became widely regarded as an essential safeguard of human life. As a result, a new group of theologians emerged who sought to revise the rule. They and others who joined them can thus rightly be called revisionists. But their movement has led to more than mere revision. It has led to destruction of the rule and a broadening of the revisionist impact to a point where questions about all species of sexual acts are being raised. Hence this book begins with a consideration of the change regarding birth control which the revisionists tried to bring about within Roman Catholicism. It discusses their attack upon that particular interpretation and application of natural law which became the accepted rule of Roman Catholic sexual ethics and which will be referred to henceforth in these pages as the natural law doctrine of human sexuality, or simply as the natural law doctrine.

Natural law theory takes a variety of approaches to the establishment of ethical rules. All seem to be rationalizations for a semi-intuitive commitment to what seems "natural" for the preservation of human culture, as we have known it, rather than rational arguments for the determination that given acts are right or wrong because they do or do not conform to what it means to be a human being, a person.

Natural law has traditionally been interpreted as being the eternal law of God for man. It is analogous to the physical laws of nature—as, for example, the law of gravity—and man, like the rest of nature, is intended to conform to it, though freely and rationally. Yet it is man's very freedom and rationality which create real difficulty; for the rest of nature behaves in accordance with natural law out of necessity, whereas man has freedom of choice. The analogy between the natural law which man is supposed to uncover rationally and choose freely, and the natural law to which the rest of nature must necessarily conform, breaks down entirely because there is no way to determine how man rationally uncovers natural law. This breakdown in the analogy is a very critical and serious one, since man's reason does *free* him to establish his own options; hence he may direct his own evolution and create his own nature—not as a static given, but as freedom ever in the process of becoming.

The revisionists' attack upon the natural law doctrine stemmed from a new understanding of sexuality and man's sexual needs, and from new developments in psychology that led to a new morality that sought the truth above everything else. Hence this is also a book about the historical reaction to the revisionist movement, about the implications of the conflict between revisionists and traditionalists, and about the way in which that conflict has affected not only sexual ethics but authority and "ecclesiastical faith" as well. It is most of all a book which points out that, despite the conflict created by the hierarchy's rejection of contraception as ethical, a sense of option prevails, at least among many theologians and perhaps among a large percentage of the world's Roman Catholics. There has been, in fact, a widespread refusal to accept the premises of the pope's recent encyclical *Humanae Vitae,* which in effect conceded nothing to those who wished to alter the traditional view of birth con-

**17**

trol. For those who would argue against that encyclical, this is a book about the necessary rethinking of the Roman Catholic sexual ethic to which refutation of the natural law doctrine leads.

The Roman Catholic sexual ethic is one which hardened into a specific understanding of "natural law" and which depended on concepts of nature, God, and a deliberate will not to interfere in the "nature" of things as God had *given* it. It is appropriate, therefore, to examine and to evaluate the historical development of that ethic in the light of man's ever-growing capability to interfere in nature (even his own), to play the godlike role of creator, and thus to direct his own evolution.

To the extent that the ethic has become an absolute, it holds within itself the seeds of its own dissolution. For it creates a terrific tension between the nature of a "law," seen to be much like one of the laws of the physical universe, and the God-given nature of the "law" of man, that is, reason. Because the tension is so great and yet in certain areas so fundamental (not merely because sexuality is fundamental but because reason and faith and ethics are), the modification or destruction of the sexual ethic could have important ramifications not only for ethics but for religious authority, faith, and even the "death" of God himself, when God is mistakenly identified with "the natural."

Many men have indeed made a god out of the natural and have used their "god" to lord it over their fellowmen. But others are finally realizing that the greatness of being man lies in being freed by the gift of reason from coming under the oppression of the "natural" in this way. Such freedom, besides being freedom from the oppression of the "natural," is thereby a freedom for openness to broader uses of one's sexual potential. It implies greater potential for living but the burden, too, of greater risk and responsibility.

It even implies (as the destruction of the old always implies) a psychic mode for viewing reality that is so novel as to bring violent reaction from those who envy and begrudge the freedoms offered to man whenever they are the result of a totally new world view and self-understanding.

In that world view freedom from oppression by the "natural" is the special gift of rational man, for reasoned reflection exposes the "natural" as, more often than not, the artificial which has been made conventional by a set of cultural and social customs and taboos. Thus an ethical decision—which is in fact a complex rational and emotional decision to act in a certain fashion—is really an individual's total assent to an idea that something represents a value for him.

To the extent that ethics is thus tied to value, it is also tied to the question of whether or not anything in this world is of value, whether or not there exists any ultimate meaning. Ethics, then, is never really separated from belief, and like belief, it is fraught with unanswerables.

Man's very existence poses for him the ultimate question of meaning, for he lives in a world that he finds unintelligible. Thirsting with an unbounded desire for life, he sees himself doomed to finitude and death. Unable to live without a purpose, he finds himself born into an existence which seems purposeless because with every passing hour it carries him another step closer toward nothingness and extinction.

When man seeks to build meaning into this kind of life, whether that meaning be ultimate or finite, he effectively (automatically) creates values. And ethics is concerned with the protection of such values. That protection must be reasonable, and hence reason is a necessary basis for morality.

It follows, then, that a question of ethics is always a question of man's highest good. Consequently, an ethical system can be developed apart from any reference to God or religion if it is directed at assisting man in the attainment of his ultimate fulfillment as a human person rather than as a creature of God as such. Ethics is thus of legitimate concern not only to the believer but to the agnostic and the atheist. However, for the believer—that is, for one who has found ultimate meaning in life—ethics poses special problems in terms of his understanding of faith, revelation, and ecclesiology. His problems vanish only if his belief includes commitment to a process of evolution relative to his understanding of these concepts.

One way of looking at the ethical systems found among Christians is to see them in a spectrum. At one end is the system of the situation ethicist who believes that love is the only norm and who therefore deems a situation's circumstances as determinative of ethical action to be based upon the norm of love (or concern). At the other end is the system of code ethics by which a situation is judged according to certain absolute principles which yield a predetermined course of ethical action.

In ethics, because the protection of certain fundamental human values is crucial, one of the most serious concerns of the Roman Catholic community ought to be the important process of singling out these values. Above all, they should be distinguished from various past, inadequate solutions to ethical problems which throughout man's history have placed such values in jeopardy. It should then be clear that, although values must be protected, the manner in which they are protected can change. A particular restriction can be eliminated when it no longer serves its intended protective purpose. In fact, its very opposite may replace it, as has already happened with the views of certain theologians regarding restrictions on contraception.

There is a certain tension between taking such "fundamental values" as normative and taking love or concern as the only norm. But there is at least as great a tension between a "fundamental value" approach and the more traditional Roman Catholic ethics which would find the solution to every problem in a rigid legalism.

A system of code ethics has two distinct drawbacks. On the one hand, an individual who must make a serious choice may often feel that his freedom to choose is denied him because he is hemmed in by the code. On the other hand he may feel that he is somehow freed by the code from the burden of responsibility for making his own ethical decision. In the latter case the code becomes a device for feeling self-satisfied; it makes the individual feel "justified" because he is following a set of prescripts. There is often little or no reflection upon the fact that these prescripts have ordinarily been designed by another fallible human being.

Situation ethics does not really remove the difficulty, for it can too easily become a convenient escape from genuine personal responsibility. The individual can delude himself into feeling that he assuming personal responsibility, even though he is doing what is convenient rather than what is really dictated by the norm of concerned Christian love. Obviously, no system is totally adequate; if one system were perfect, there would be no spectrum. And there can be no perfect system because of the very nature of man which is susceptible to change. Therefore all values—except the non-revaluable one of existence itself—are subject to change and reassessment.

For any understanding of ethics, man's rational nature is a determining factor. Man is the only creature on earth who is rational, and it is this rationality which characterizes his nature.[1] Whatever may be his final ethical decision in a given situation, his options must first of all be rational, that is, they must be in harmony with his nature as a person. From this starting point one might conclude either that man is somewhat restricted in his ethical choices or that his ethical choices are on that basis rather elastic. For moral choices based on a given nature ought to be clear-cut and simple unless that given nature is not so "given" or fixed and finite but, instead, flexible and susceptible to infinite variety and mutation.

Here the link between ethics and faith must be remembered, for man's paradoxical nature is the source, not only of his ethical dilemma, but of his religious quest as well. Faith is the dynamic relation between man and God; through it, man seeks to approach God, despite the unsolvable mystery of what God is. And because God does remain always a mystery, man can attempt to approach him more closely by exploring the knowable element in the man-God relationship —namely, man. By knowing man, the creature made in God's own image, one approaches God.

The image of God in man is man's unbounded capacity, his rationality. And that rationality is also the critical defining factor about man. Hence, if there is a natural law of man, it must begin at least with the human process whereby man reasons to the acceptance of one or more options for the resolution of any situation of conflict. Ethical decision is then firmly predicated on reasonable argument, rather than on arbitrary convention or tradition outmoded but maintained through religious submission of reason to unreasonable authority.

The Christian's most fundamental commitment is with the question of faith, the basic and central concern of religion, the inexhaustible source of theological speculation. His reason for believing that he will approach the mystery of God by an understanding of the nature of man is twofold: He knows that man is created in God's image, and he knows that the concrete result of the faith relationship from the point of view of man is to come closer to an understanding of God. He can come to know God through knowing himself, by coming to a greater self-consciousness, a greater self-awareness, and for this reason he wants to know what it means to be a human person, to exist, to have life. Struggle toward God, "religious" quest, is thus yearning for and evolution towards self-knowledge, not in the psychoanalytic sense but in the sense of discovering what fulfills the potential of man, what fulfills the individual. This discovery is part of God's revelation of what man is, and therefore of what God is. To carry out this quest, rationality is man's principal tool and faith his vehicle.

Implicit in faith in Jesus is the element of trust. A great contribution of Protestantism to Christianity is the emphasis placed upon the Christian's trust in Christ which holds that though man is a sinner, he is yet justified. If the notion has any genuine validity of an existential nature relative to faith and morals, it is that we are never certain when we act out our faith in a really radical way—that is, on the ethical level —that we can enjoy moral complacency. We must criticize those who relieve themselves of responsibility by following another person, or even a code, and then say, "We did only what we were told."

Every significant ethical choice involves a genuine risk and is thus related to faith because we must trust Jesus. One risks all to gain all. One risks even Christ's love to grow in Christ's image, and trusts that Christ's love is sufficient to the situation. The hardest moral choices are not those where choices are unclear, because they can only be based on irresolvable dilemmas of science or law; rather, the difficulty lies in those choices which are in fact clear but which the individual must make utterly on his own. He must then take the risk upon himself, shoulder the responsibility, and take up the burden, but always in the trusting knowledge that Jesus has already taken up the cross of our sins and has thereby given meaning to our efforts.

In the context of a new world view, the Roman Catholic sexual ethic seems a product of taboo and fear and, consequently, the expression of a prejudice rather than of a conviction of reason. The sexual ethic thus seems to distort values rather than to protect them. For example, there is no clear-cut, supposedly intrinsic or "natural" reason why being monogamous, as opposed to being polygamous, is any more virtuous than having been born with blue eyes instead of brown. No normative ethical valuation, either positive or negative, can be automatically placed upon either monogamy or polygamy; for everything that is known about man's nature inclines one to conclude that to identify "the natural" with "normalcy" is to yield to a totally perverse understanding of what man's *nature* really is. To say that polygamy is wrong because it violates the natural law is to beg the question: It is merely to say that it is wrong because it is wrong.

If such an action is wrong, there must be a reason why it is wrong. If it violates the natural law, there must be a reason why it does so. Yet no such reason seems to exist. Because so much of the natural law sexual morality suffers from this difficulty, one suspects other motivations for ethical decisions—perhaps a fear of social consequences or simply a fear of sexuality and its potential for evil abuse. To live in fear of one's sexuality, however, is like living in fear of having an appendix. One might indeed be betrayed by being a sexed person; but it makes as little sense to regulate one's life, or a large segment of it, by fear of the effects of being sexed as it does by fear of appendicitis.

If there is one objective of this book, it is to replace the terror of taboo and restriction with a commonsense, closer approximation of real life; to replace negativism with a joyful openness toward life, toward love, toward being, and toward all that is positive—in a word, toward all that *is*.

To say that there is no intrinsic moral valuation in any species of sexual act is to say that moral valuation of any act derives from the context of an individual's life, not from an abstract code, not even from an abstract judgment of particular circumstances; rather, the valuation derives from the personal judgment of the individual who is willing to respond to the rational freedom which defines his very humanity and who, instead of shrinking in cowardice and fear from that responsibility, welcomes the opportunity to share with his God the burden of cooperation in the creation of himself.

What cannot be overlooked here is the whole spirit that is at stake. It is the spirit of reason opposing taboo, where taboo—based largely on fear of what might happen to human life, societies, culture, and institutions if time-honored routes to human fulfillment are altered—has been disguised as nature (God). It is a kind of death of God. Above all, it is the death of orthodoxy. It is equivalent to rejection of the static which alone permits even the notion of orthodoxy. It is a rejection of the ghetto religious mentality which maintains that somehow the ghetto groups are unique, that they are God's chosen ones and have a monopoly on rightness; for such a mentality is a corollary only of static doctrinality.

This book, then, is a plea for life. It rejects the creation of a sham god who can live only at the expense of reason, freedom, and life, which is the very stuff of humanity, at least the stuff of humans truly made in God's image. It rejects the guilt imposed from without upon a conscience formed, not by man before God at the risk of personal free decision but rather by man molded by authority, which is simply the abnegation of our God-given human responsibility and freedom in exchange for the traitor's coin of neurotic security from the anxiety of being human.

For those who think the negativism, the terror, the anxiety, and the guilt are overstated, it should suffice merely to reflect upon the spirit and the letter of the commonly used manuals of moral theology. They represent a total domination of the field by a universally accepted set of restrictions predicated upon a universally accepted theological attitude toward sexual ethics. If anything, then, this present book is a religious rejection of guilt where there should be no guilt.

The goal of this work, then, will be to talk about human sexuality and its morality as it exists in reality and, by so talking, to say something about how man relates to it morally or immorally.

Human sexuality has been discussed for a number of years during the so-called sexual revolution. Concern with the subject has existed on a number of levels, including the ethical; for human beings have long felt that sexuality, because it is a significant part of human life, carries with it significant potential for dangerous moral abuses.

One cannot, however, talk about a new Catholic sexual ethic apart from at least a brief sketch of its historical development. Sexual problems are with us even today, but a reexamination of the past, augmented by new insights that have come to us particularly through psychology and through the improved communications of our technologically advanced age, can perhaps offer better solutions. Certainly rapid change has radically altered man's outlook on human sexuality, so one can try to seize as many insights as modern scientific developments offer and add these to the knowledge of the past. The goal can then be to create a new fundamental view of sexuality; to tackle more realistically, more truthfully, and in a more Christian manner, the very deep problems which have remained essentially unsolved; and to present a more profound, more Christian, and more truthful description of what human life—which is sexed life—requires for the ethical use of one's sexual potential.

Certain past justifications for a book on the ethics of human sexuality are no longer germane. Few, if any, modern men long for a learned statement offering infallible guidelines for the sinless use of one's sexual powers in keeping with the rules and regulations of the Church. On the contrary, one can only hope to suggest a new theological approach to reality based upon a new world view and therefrom to present some reflections upon what might serve as reasonable guidelines for the Christian, human, rational use of sexuality.

But why even this? Is there some great threat to which this work is a response? No. However, this book may fill the gap that exists among printed works by Roman Catholic moral theologians. For it is difficult to find in print a modern treatment of the role of sexuality in human life from a strictly theological point of view. There is a new morality today based upon an insistence that life be meaningful, and that meaning can best come from doing what is right for the humanistic evolution of the race towards the betterment of each individual's lot. One might indeed credit this insistence to contemporary "youth," for they make up the new generation that insists on a new morality. But it is inadequate to attribute their insistence to their youthfulness. And it is misleading, for successive generations have always seemed wayward to their parents; yet they have always functioned to preserve the status quo. What is unique about so many of those born after 1935, and about those older people as well who are able to reject the posture of the closed mind, is that they have made an evolutionary leap to a new world view. They have not merely liberalized a few accidentals of human laws and life. They have substantially altered the very context of human life by their ability to embrace a totally new understanding of its structure. This new morality stems from a conviction that the individual has tremendous value and that his needs must be responded to here and now. To do anything less is to be inhuman. To be inhuman is immoral. And so the new morality is really a thrust toward behaving at our human best, and where sex is concerned, the modern man will consider reasonable guidelines for the moral use of this potential just as he will consider those pertaining to the moral use of all human potential.

Man's search for meaning is a search for moral relevance, for growth to self-consciousness as person. In a certain sense what is more personal, more intimately involved with interpersonal relationships than the fact of one's sexuality and the uses to which one puts it? It is too simple to dismiss the role of sexuality in human life as either incidental, extraneous, or minimal. If such were the case, Freud could scarcely have developed the master science of the twentieth century. No, sexuality is in no way irrelevant in the lives of men. And yet, though its importance has been overstressed in connection with such trivialities as anatomical measurements, there has been a complete failure to properly emphasize, discuss, and inquire about it in those areas in which it is of vital importance, such as its relation to proper psychosexual development. This book may serve to dispel certain false theological notions and to build up sound theological opinion that can serve constructively as guidelines upon which those committed to the growth of human persons and their fulfillment can count for healthy and productive moral suggestions.

Light bends as it passes through certain media. Truth bends as it passes through a given time period. The modern dissenting Catholic is a man who insists that, without wanting to insert himself into the truth in an antiauthoritarian fashion, he must nevertheless stand up and declare his rejection on rational grounds of any attempt, in the name of false gods, to hold back man's progressive evolution towards the true God.

Luther saw injustice and immorality in the Church, and he protested against it in the name of Jesus—as he understood his faith commitment to Jesus. Interestingly, the nature of Luther's protest was such that it struck at the fundamental commitment, or commitment to ultimacy, of persons who could not or would not revise their understanding of that commitment.

Even today there are individuals whose faith is not really in God or even in religion, but in their own brand of theology. These are the orthodoxians; their faith is in theology and doctrine—not in God, but in statements of man about God. They will respect the agnostic or unbeliever, but they reject the position of the believer who articulates or understands his commitment in a different universe of theological discourse from theirs. These men are imprisoned in the bag of orthodoxy. They are obsolete, and they are expendable.

The conflict over the issue of contraception is an indication that the Church's children have grown up. Evidences of this growth are the problems currently being experienced with respect to authority and faith. Authority dies when it becomes irrelevant. This happens in a context of innovation when authority is based not on the stability of reason but on the stability of an absence of change. For the latter is not a viable human stability at all, but rather sheer instability in an age of rapid change. The process of modernization, radicalization of life-style, or democratization means a turning away from the static and a presumption that everything can be rethought. There are no commitments on the part of modern man to anything less than the paradox-sprung dialectic itself. In ethics this means innovation, because it means the rejection of the idea that there is a given, static norm predicated upon the customary, the normal, or the traditional. The man with a mind-set is indeed obsolete, a creature of another era.

He is today's antiman, since the pace of contemporary change is too rapid to run the risk of commitment to error. We may indeed be entering the age of the uncommitted man, for modern man would prefer to remain uncommitted, and hence unfulfilled, than to stake his life on what might be an error. He places too much value on life's meaning to allow commitment to anything but ultimacy.

## Footnotes 1

1. The relation between a religious ethical system and man's rationality calls to mind a serious prior question concerning the role of reason in matters of ethics and religion. That question concerns the problem of the relation between the rational and the nonrational in human life, which is analogous to that between reason and faith. Taking the stand that all truth is one, I feel the believer must accept the total and absolute, noncontradictory validity of the truths of both faith and reason. I likewise proceed from the premise that, despite the contribution of belief-statements to the problems of ethics, there should be neither contradiction nor, in fact, disparity between the ethics of the believer and the nonbeliever, as it is my conviction that ethical judgments—even when enlightened by the message of faith—do not exceed the limits of comprehension of reason as it probes the evolving nature of man in an effort to determine how that nature is best fulfilled.

# 2
# THE HISTORICAL BACKGROUND AND THE FINAL RULE

The heritage of the modern Catholic in the matter of sexual ethics is an attitude. Characterized by legalistic hair-splitting, it is a product of a tradition which, despite certain innovations, has been consistent over a considerable period of time. The attitude is one of concern with sins and with the effort to delineate as many kinds of sin as possible. Looking at that heritage, one cannot help but feel that the time has come for a new morality based not on an unreasoned subservience to syllogisms now outdated, but upon reasonable conclusions grounded in humane logic and vastly improved science.

## The First Half of this Century

The idea that it is a mortal sin to kiss another person's arm may sound preposterous. This, however, is the inescapable syllogistic conclusion of a confessors' manual which has been so popular that it has gone through no less than eighteen editions. In the eighteenth English edition of this work, *Moral Theology*,[1] published in 1963, its popularity is pointed out and the claim made that it has been adapted to the laws and customs of the United States.

One of the admonitions in the work is that all directly voluntary sexual pleasure outside the married state is mortally sinful, even if the pleasure be ever so brief and insignificant; it is sinful because the manner in which the pleasure is sought is believed to frustrate the natural purpose of sexuality. The author emphasizes that there is no lightness of matter[2] in the area of sexual pleasure. He maintains that the sinfulness of a situation lies in the pleasure it affords, and then goes on to itemize as many instances (and there are an astonishing number) of potential sin as possible.

We are told, for example, that directly voluntary masturbation is always a mortal sin; but that it is lawful for an individual to wash himself, to go bathing, and to ride, even though he knows that, because of his particular reaction to these situations, "pollution" will result. It is also lawful to seek relief from itching in the sex organs, provided that the cause of discomfort is not excessive semen or ardent passion. (He displays leniency in this case, though, and says that should one have doubts about the cause of the itching, he may go ahead and relieve it anyway.) Also, it is lawful to relieve slight itching if only minor sexual stimulation is experienced therefrom. In all these instances, however, the supposition is that one does not consent to any venereal pleasure; otherwise, one commits sin.

All areas even remotely related to sexual pleasure are combed in an effort to uncover additional fertile ground for yet more sins. We are told that the action of distillation, which is described as the emission of the subtle nonprolific urethral fluid (the purpose of which is to facilitate the ejection of the semen), may or may not be sinful. If there is no sexual pleasure, then distillation is no sin. However, if distillation is accompanied by venereal pleasure, it is a sin of the same gravity and species as pollution.

Absorption with the delineation of sexual sins leads to some humorous subdivisions. The reader learns, for example, that even sodomy has its imperfections. Father Jone defines sodomy as unnatural copulation with either a person of the same sex—in which case it is called perfect sodomy—or with a person of the opposite sex—in which case it is called imperfect sodomy (rectal intercourse). For the ultimate in sexual sin, nothing surpasses bestiality, the coition of a human being with an animal. It does not matter in what manner the act is performed, for the malice resides in the perverted attitude towards the animal. Bestiality is the worst of all the sins of impurity.

The search for sin is carried to the extreme of irrationality with a great concern for what is, biologically speaking, a more or less automatic physical response of the body to something over which one has little, if any, control. Jone defines what he calls sexual commotion as the pleasurable disturbance, or excitement, of the genital organs and the fluid that serves the purpose of generation. He holds that any directly voluntary sexual commotion may be a mortal sin if the action causing it exercises by its nature a great influence on the stimulation of the sexual appetite. He warns that if a voluntary superfluous action is the cause of the agitation, one must offer resistance by desisting from the action. Failure to do so is gravely sinful if the action strongly tends by its nature to carnal lust. Were the influence slight, only a venial sin would be committed; but if one voluntarily engaged in such an action for any length of time, then the sin generally would become grievous because of the great danger of giving consent. Such concern seems to point to a preference for denying the physical, animal aspects of one's humanity. It seems almost like a rejection of God's handiwork in favor of a perverse desire to be superhuman or angelic.

The cataloguing of sins in the area of specific concrete actions is delineated in the finest detail and covers the full range of actions that are even remotely connected to sexuality from childhood to the time of engagement to marry. The emphasis is always on sin; where mortal ones cannot be found, venial ones can often be uncovered. For example, Father Jone is gravely concerned with the external sins against modesty. Though, as we have seen, he allows the touching of one's private parts in bathing, or for healing purposes, or to relieve irritation, he holds that children should be taught to refrain entirely from touching their genital organs. He declares that it is seriously sinful to touch without reason the private parts of other persons of either sex, even over their clothing. But he acknowledges that such touches would be only venially sinful if they were done in a hasty or casual manner and without evil intention, and out of levity. Touching animals indecently is gravely sinful if it is done for a long time, or if the animal suffers pollution.

The author holds that ardent, prolonged, and repeated kissing is often a mortal sin, though he excepts such kissing and embracing between parents and children. However, to kiss the arms or legs or back or breast is gravely sinful.

We are told that it is lawful to look at the private parts of one's own body if there is a reasonable cause for doing so. To do so out of curiosity or levity would be venially sinful. It is also venially sinful to glance at the private parts of other persons of the same sex, but it is not wrong to look at their semiprivate parts unless it is done with sodomitical intentions. Provided that no sexual pleasure is aroused by observing animals mating, one commits only a venial sin when one watches out of curiosity.

Jone offers us the thought that going steady with the intention of early marriage may be looked upon as a necessary occasion of sin. He holds that those intending to marry should avoid, as far as possible, being alone. He also holds that they should not be together too often but, when they are, they are forbidden to do anything which is not permitted to other single people. They may touch, embrace, or kiss each other in a becoming manner; but they may not consent to sexual pleasure that might be caused thereby.

Interestingly enough, Jone's work is characteristic of the principal works in the field which were widely used in seminaries as the standard textbooks for courses in moral theology. It is cited here merely as an example of theological manuals in general. Those manuals treat sexual sins so similarly that they often read as though they were written by the same author. They are critical to our study, for they represent the high-water mark, the climax, in an uninterrupted development of the legalistic treatment of sexual ethics. They were the textbooks used in moral theology courses in seminaries through the entire first half of this century and even into the sixties; and they went virtually unchallenged until the present period. They illustrate how firmly entrenched, how pervasive, and how thoroughly accepted was the attitude from which they had sprung. And, even if the ordinary layman was totally unaware of their existence and might not understand much of their vocabulary, he was—by reason of the attitude toward sexuality which had been inculcated in him—well schooled in obedience to their requirements.

In one moral theology textbook widely used in seminaries there is added to the same discussion the warning that the observance of human coitus is a mortal sin if such observance is not brief enough or, however brief, if it is not from a great enough distance.[3] If these conditions of time and distance are observed, however, there would not be mortal sin. The general gist of the thinking, as previously pointed out, is that outside of marriage mortal sin is always committed whenever venereal pleasure is directly sought or deliberately consented to, no matter how slight the venereal excitement may be. 1565862

Even in the case of simple fornication—that is, intercourse between an unmarried man and an unmarried woman —there is a feeling that it is somehow against nature. A third, very popular, author holds that although fornication is said to be the sin that is consummated according to the natural mode, it is really repugnant to human nature.[4] His reason is that we must not consider natural merely that which we have in common with the beast, but rather we must consider natural to man that which is rational; and fornication for him is not rational. Clearly there is an underlying assumption here that the sexual organs are ordained specifically and intrinsically for the generation of the human species and for nothing else.

All these authors see lust as the inordinate seeking of venereal pleasure. And the inordinateness stems directly from the ways in which the use of sexuality is disoriented from the proper generative act which is marital as well as heterosexual and procreation-oriented. What strikes one most particularly in all these works is that page after page is devoted to the most minute distinctions concerning internal and external sins against the virtues of modesty, purity, and chastity in connection with thoughts, looks, touches, songs, occasions of sin. One wonders how so much ink could have been spilled on such topics. Father Bernard Haring, writing as late as 1963, is careful to distinguish between mortal and venial sins and to hold that sins against purity—typical sins of weakness—exclude those who commit them from attaining the kingdom of God.[5] And he holds firmly to the teaching that such sins are objectively grave ones.

Certainly contemporary psychological insights and rapid changes in social structure and attitudes are influencing many younger priests and seminarians today. Yet the reactionary character of *Humanae Vitae* and the statements of some of the national hierarchies make one wonder how much, if at all, official Church teaching has changed. Some theological seminaries still follow a traditional line of thinking in their teaching of moral theology. Where professors labor under the requirements that texts be approved by the Roman Congregations, the teaching is therefore still quite conservative, if not reactionary.

This situation is reflected in priestly attitudes on the

practical level. Some priests, whose pastoral approach is one of great leniency in the confessional, have not really budged on the theoretical level. Making a valiant effort to adjust to rapid changes, some priests defend the pope's *Humanae Vitae* while showing great compassion for those practicing contraception. This almost schizoid pattern, made in an effort at adjustment, is leaving many priests with feelings of guilt about the confessional advice they are giving. It is a reflection of poor seminary training, and it is causing so much pressure that in some instances priests are abandoning their priesthood.

Overall, however, and particularly in the light of the recent encyclical, the structure of the present teaching in the Church is such that a Catholic's attitude on contraception is likely to be an excellent yardstick of his total attitude toward ethical problems of a sexual nature generally.

And it is interesting that the individual's attitude toward sexuality is very much what is at issue here. From a sociological viewpoint, attitude is even more powerful than law. While laws to be complied with remain on the books, attitude is part and parcel of an individual's very being. Attitude is part of the milieu in which the child is reared; it determines to a large extent one's identification with his family, his peer groups, and the other institutions which comprise the basic structure of his society. Attitudes are ingrained; they are automatic. Moreover, from a religious viewpoint, law is intended to shape attitude and to do so absolutely and definitively. Even so, laws themselves are delineated more precisely because of attitudes. There is thus a circular effect operative in the relationship between law and attitude.

One of the past difficulties in using religious restrictions as a means of control was that sexuality in general was taken too seriously. This manifested itself in the contention on the part of theologians that there was no lightness of matter where sexuality was concerned. Besides making grave matter out of light matter, however, the attitude engendered by the adoption of this means of control amounted to a distorted understanding of the true role of sexuality in human life. But the gravest error lay not in the means used as means—they may have been the best that humans could muster at the time. Most serious was the fact that intrinsic to the means was a concept of absoluteness which left no room for evolution of the rule relative to augmented knowledge.

When one encounters authors who are so preoccupied with the escape from sexuality that they squander their time in telling the reader that it is not sinful to wash the private parts of one's body, one is tempted to wonder: What is the psychological integrity of any individual who would pose, even to himself, the question of whether or not such an act should be permitted? One is further pressed to question the attitude of an author whose approach is not merely negative, but destructive, in that it renders sexuality suspect. What must be his underlying psychological and existential attitude if he sees matters of this kind in such a light, and deals lengthily and seriously with fine-line legalistic distinctions about the quality of individual, isolated acts of a sexual nature? Why, too, do authors see the specific evil involved in venereal acts as resting in pleasure? What is the source of this antipleasure attitude? Why is it specifically the pleasure that is the source of the evil? Why do authors say that all directly voluntary sexual pleasure outside wedlock is greviously sinful? What causes any author to adopt the attitude that pleasure is, or can be, grievously sinful?

Outlines can be found concerning pleasure that is complete, pleasure that is incomplete, pleasure that is directly voluntary, pleasure that is indirectly voluntary, sins that are external, sins that are internal; others deal with thoughts, phantasms, deliberate complacency, morose delectation, conversation, songs, nudism. How could this view, which is almost perverted in its preoccupation with sexuality as a major sin, exist? From a psychological viewpoint it seems close to being pathological. Does the obsession with sexual sin serve as a distraction from something else which threatens great anxiety? What is the origin of this apparent fear of sexuality? Where did such unanimity of hostile feeling about it originate? The answers, if based upon human evolution from the beginning of time, may indeed be beyond us. But let us examine at least the basic sources within the Christian tradition out of which this attitude toward sex developed. For it was to that attitude, with all of its vigor and absolutism, that the entire Catholic world had submitted.

## The Ancient Background

The development of medieval attitudes toward human sexuality owed much to the moral principles found in the New Testament, and in particular to the guidance of Saint Paul and his influence on the Fathers.

The early Christians were aware that their discipleship depended upon asceticism and self-sacrifice. A man had to be ready to leave all in order to follow Christ; even a wife was an encumbrance in the service of the Lord.

The first Christians wanted to know what marriage and sexuality meant for them; it became Saint Paul's task to reply to their questions, and his words have echoed through the centuries. He has been labeled by some as reactionary and by others as inspired, but all would agree that his influence has been both deep and lasting.

Much of what Saint Paul wrote about sex and marriage is universally acceptable, and by the standards of his time his insight into the meaning of human sexuality is extraordinary. But Paul never set out to write a treatise on the subject. His treatment was neither comprehensive nor systematic; he was merely responding with practical solutions to practical questions addressed to him by the brethren who were seeking to make their discipleship valid and wholehearted. Moreover, he was writing to the Corinthians, a dissolute people notorious for their sexual licentiousness.

Paul's message, therefore, is complex. He spoke of love and of sex in realistic terms, charging husband and wife with the responsibility of donation of themselves to one another.

And he described the love between husband and wife as analogous to that between Christ and the Church. He asked husbands and wives to love and reverence their spouses as they would their own bodies, even, in fact, as the Lord loves the Church. Paul thus suggested a beautiful description of marriage in the plan of Redemption. He made coitus a means of total expression of the person in communication and commitment.

Yet, although he insisted upon the spiritual equality of man and woman in Christ, he yielded to the male-centered attitudes underpinning the social structures of his time. Seeing God, Christ, man, and woman in a descending order of subordination, he fitted the marital relationship into this pattern, asking wives to submit themselves to their husbands in everything as they would to the Lord. He explained that the husband is the head of the wife as Christ is the head of the Church.

Paul was certainly doing no more than yielding to the customs of his time; but, as history would have it, with the adoption of the Canon it was an easy step to the canonization of the author's personal attitudes as such. The effect, unfortunately, was to yield a theological (scriptural) basis for the status of woman as beneath that of man, despite New Testament assurances of the equality of male and female in Christ.

The influence of another of Paul's personal attitudes left him open to a gross misinterpretation of his meaning. It proved to have most severe consequences for the Church. Paul expected the *parousia* at any moment, and a true understanding of his position requires a degree of empathy for the eschatological pressure under which he lived and thought and wrote. Clearly, Paul made no secret of his preference for the single state; but it was "because of the present distress" and because "the time is short" and because a marriage partner is thus a hindrance to the service of the Lord.

Paul added to his personal preference (that virgins and widows remain single) the command that those who cannot remain continent do better to marry than to burn with passion. But his making of marriage a condescension to human weakness was really an enlightened, liberal position when seen against the background of an imminent Second Coming of Christ. Marriage became a logical, humane means whereby those not able to remain continent until the Lord came could avoid fornications. Paul, in addition to not concealing his preference for virginity, idealized it. But, again, his attitude toward marriage was not reactionary; in the context of his thought, it was quite liberal.

The ascetical balance of Paul's words was nevertheless weighted beyond question in favor of the single state. Virginity was exalted as a religious ideal. In an ascetically oriented age Paul's words (removed from their eschatological context) would surely be misunderstood. In such an age the Apostle's insights into marital love could easily be passed over in favor of his description of virginal service as representative of the consecrated spirit preferable to the divided spirit of the wed. The Patristic was such an age.

As with Paul, the Patristic treatment of human sexuality was never comprehensive or systematic; it consisted mainly in the occasional, practical rather than speculative, treatment of principles in response to particular questions or controversies. Not given to crystal-clear, balanced exposition, the Fathers generally attempted to harmonize the acceptable mores of their milieus with their understanding of the Scriptures and the Christian life.

With the exception of Tertullian and Jerome, the Fathers did not denigrate marriage as much as—impelled by the powerful ascetical enthusiasm of the day—they idealized sexual continence (virginity, widowhood, retreat to celibacy in monastery or desert). Continence was considered the ultimate mark of the disciplined ascetic who has attained the perfection of self-denial and mortification of the flesh.

One can find the Fathers speaking in defense of marriage, but in general they depicted it as a rather bleak prospect. Engrossed as they were with the physical aspects of sexual activity, especially coitus, their orientation was highly biological. Their considerations were with sex acts considered precisely as discrete acts, and their approach was to be that of the majority of Roman Catholic moralists well into the twentieth century. The Pauline ideal of virginal service was seen as a "higher life" at the expense of marriage, which was analyzed mainly in terms of the discrete-act morality. Obviously sexuality was accorded no value in this arrangement in which there was a strong antipleasure element.

The use of sexuality even when limited legitimately to the married state was distasteful, as it suggested an affliction, a deficiency, a weakness—specifically, an inability to remain continent. It thus had a bad connotation and was in need of justification. The Fathers were led to find the justification of marital coitus in the good of procreation, although it should be noted that there is a certain inconsistency in this view even in Augustine. He himself would prefer the hastening of the end of the world through virginal abstinence. Yet, since some persons cannot be continent, they are permitted marital intercourse. The intercourse is licit, however, not because it satisfies their passions but because by it they intend to produce offspring.

Augustine is an important psychological study, for his influence on the development of the Church's attitudes toward sexuality was the most profound of all the Fathers and the most lasting. He saw sex tainted with evil because an element of evil was present in every act of intercourse; that evil element was lustful passion (*libido*). The evil was made tolerable, however, by marriage, provided that the sex act was performed expressly for the sake of procreation or for the rendering of the marital debt. This notion was to be for centuries the guiding rule of Roman Catholic thinking about coitus. In it is synthesized the Patristic deprecation of marriage as second-rate—a condescension to incontinence—and the view that coitus, even in marriage, is rendered sinless only by reason of counterbalancing goods: offspring or justice.

This view of Augustine's resulted from his emotional need to resolve the tension he felt between his own experience of sex and the chaste ideal of which it fell short. He had practiced coitus in an eleven-year concubinage, which turned out to be an interesting approximation of marriage but an experience profoundly steeped in unhappiness and guilt. As oriented toward lustful gratification as the relationship was, from Augustine's viewpoint at least, this "approximation of marriage" seemed to lack the desire for children (there was only one child in eleven years), and faithfulness cemented and insured by the permanent bond of matrimony (he left the girl to satisfy his mother). The effect on Augustine was a turning toward offspring and permanent fidelity as central elements in his ideal of the married state.

At the same time Augustine's philosophical search for truth, especially religious truth, had led him to a powerful rejection of his own commitment to Manicheism, particularly the Manichean religious doctrine of the evil of procreation. The tension generated by his rebellion against the Manichean antimarriage doctrine on the one hand and his own ideal of sexual continence on the other apparently led him to embrace the Stoic ideal which accepted sexual intercourse, but only as a means to procreation.

For Augustine personally, the resolution of his difficulties came only with his conversion to a life of complete celibacy. However, in his condescension to the married—that is, to those who could not remain continent—he was totally unable to accept contraceptive coitus, even though this could have hastened the coming of the kingdom of God. Instead his powerful emotional and intellectual rejection of the Manichean doctrine hardened his insistence that the justification of an individual's consent to wedlock, that is, to his inability to remain continent, should be that thereby children are raised up to God.

If Augustine was principally responsible for the propagation in Christian thought of the idea that sex is somehow tainted with evil, it was Gregory the Great who introduced the idea that the peculiar evil of human sexuality lay not in the concupiscence (as Saint Augustine had said) but in the pleasure of coitus. Thus marital intercourse would be sinful if pleasure rather than procreation were the motivation for it. The importance of this view cannot be overlooked, because the role of pleasure in sexual intercourse—especially in the light of the then influential Aristotelian position that virtue lies in the median or mean dictated by right reason—would be significant for the medieval discussion of sex ethics and would remain so into the twentieth century.

The status of women is important in any attempt at understanding sexual mores. Even in Paul, who asserted the relative unimportance of sexual differences in the context of life in Christ (Gal. 3:28), woman was created for man's benefit and was subject to him. This very fundamental, male-centered attitude accounts for a Patristic dualism much like our own double standard, and goes a long way toward explaining why there could be such a difference in the treatment of male and female sexuality (for instance, widowhood and virginity are really seen as primarily female virtues).

Nevertheless a real ambivalence toward women is confirmed by the fact that, despite their lower status, widows, virgins, and deaconesses were accorded a special place in the official Church structure, although their service was limited and more the result of what was needed than what the given episcopal structure required.

Just as the Church presumed even from New Testament times to compose responses appropriate to the practical needs of the community, so too it exercised what it believed to be its ordinary right to legislate measures appropriate to the good order of the Church, partly because there was no other regulatory force in many periods. In sexual matters a number of different documents provide basically the same kind of prohibition against fornication, adultery, digamy, abortion, homosexuality, divorce, rape, bigamy, the fall or marriage of virgins, desertion, bestiality, and incest.

In a word, the Patristic period was profoundly characterized by negativism when it came to placing value on human sexuality. Despite numerous changes that would creep into Patristic doctrines in succeeding centuries, this negativism was to become only more evident.

The asceticism of the age reacted to Paul's guidelines with an abhorrence of sexuality. Suspected of being evil, sexuality was deplored as a sign of weakness, an inability to keep continent, a lack of self-denial. This in turn encouraged a new kind of asceticism in which morbid preoccupation with sexuality set an extraordinary value on mortification of the flesh by means of various kinds of abstinence from venereal indulgence[6] and even abstinence from interest in things in any way connected with the venereal.[7] As a result marriage was depreciated to a low level, regarded as little more than an acceptable condescension to lust. Virginity was exalted above marriage, even though it was marriage, not virginity, which was a sacrament instituted and blessed by God. The Patristic penchant was to play up the trials, difficulties, and discomforts of marriage, and to play down its joys, consolations, and rewards.

The sacredness of marriage, nevertheless, was defended against those who would sanction promiscuity or adultery; and the permanence of the marriage bond was held against those who would advocate divorce. Moreover, if marriage was the acceptable framework within which venereal activities could be carried out, nonmarital venereal indulgence was strictly forbidden.

What seems most interesting in Saint Augustine and in the general Patristic view of human sexuality is that while marriage and intercourse were justified only for the particular reason that they produced offspring, no figure of influence ever suggested marriage for the sake of the joys and pleasures of family life. Further, the fact that sex and marriage were recommended for those who could not remain continent seems to say a good deal about how the Fathers viewed their universe. It seems that they saw sexuality as a thorn in the flesh of human life. One can well understand Augustine's connection of concupiscible sex with the Fall of man. Surely he saw the Fall more as man's descent from his natural state to an unfortunate subnatural state, than from an above-natural state to his natural state. In an Augustinian universe of this sort, then, man would always be at odds with himself since he would always be dealing with his present nature as not merely "fallen," in the sense of needing improvement, but as somehow not his proper nature at all. The psychological implications, as history has demonstrated, would be significant.

## The Medieval Background

The sexual concerns of the medieval period were more concentrated than in the Patristic period. The question of divorce and the possibility of remarriage afterward became more important in the early Middle Ages. During the Dark Ages, as this period has been called, considerable controversy arose over divorce and remarriage; and it was not until the eleventh century that the reforming influence of Gregory VII (Hildebrand) effected a universal return to the position that divorce and remarriage were strictly forbidden.

It was at this time that the Pauline privilege was interpreted to mean that not only separation but even subsequent remarriage of the converted spouse was permissible.[8] This touched off a debate over indissolubility, because account had to be taken of the early Church tradition that the union of pagans was, in some sense at least, indissoluble.

The discussion led to the more important medieval question of what the requirements were for a valid marriage. There was no real departure from the Pauline evaluation of the states of chastity: virginity, widowhood, marriage. If anything, the exaltation of virginity to the level of a superideal of human life was only strengthened by Hildebrand's movement toward strict enforcement of clerical celibacy.[9] But marriage did assume a special importance which it had not previously had, mainly as a result of the Church's gaining sole jurisdiction in matrimonial cases. The emphasis, however, was on the legalistic aspects of matrimony rather than on a theology of sex. Even in Thomas Aquinas, who had some notions about the personal aspects of marriage, the Aristotelian rationalism of the period left the question of love untreated in connection with the married state, since it appeared to be outside the bounds of theological and philosophical speculation. Thus the personal side of marriage was neglected, and the resulting theology of marriage was highly juridical. So was the social attitude toward it.

Discussion centered on the functions of mutual donation and consummation (first intercourse) in the establishment of a valid and hence indissoluble union. The critical question was whether or not intercourse was an essential part of marriage.[10] A number of conflicting views, some requiring coitus for validity, others not requiring it, can be found; yet often no precise explanation of why one position or another is held accompanies them. In any case the position that mutual donation effected the sacrament triumphed because ecclesiastical tribunals ultimately needed a simple (obvious, external, public) test of the validity of marriage.

The Middle Ages found sexual intercourse suspect, and the influence of Gregory's position—that its evil lay in the pleasure associated with it—caused concern over the sinfulness of coitus even in marriage. Albert the Great saw its evil in the ability of its pleasurableness to distract man's Fall-weakened reason from contemplation.

This idea is clearly akin to Augustine's contention that the lustful passion involved in intercourse caused a loss of reason; and therein lay the evil of the act. It is not strange then that Albert's pupil, Thomas Aquinas, for whom Augustine was a theological master, would amplify this idea. Moreover, Aquinas, whose influence beyond the Middle Ages far surpassed that of all other medieval theologians combined, was very much impressed by Aristotle's doctrine concerning virtue; he thus saw evil in anything that could in any way hinder the proper use of right reason.

This preoccupation with the evil of human sexuality was certainly nothing new to Christian thought in the West, as we have already seen. Yet certainly its importance for an understanding of medieval thought cannot be overestimated. The medieval discussions of marriage as such were far more enlightened than the Patristic discussions, and the value and goodness of marriage were vindicated by heavy emphasis on the place of marriage as a sacrament. But the old aversion, fear, and suspicion of the sexual act itself remained, and the clerical model supported certain notions such as the power of sexuality to draw one's attention from the contemplation of divine things.

Against such a background, little discussion of a positive role of sex—for example, in love—was possible. Wary of sex, concerned with ecclesiastical law, and devoted to Aristotelian realism, the theologians set down rules of human sexual behavior elaborated in detailed scholastic fashion from their Patristic heritage. The Fathers had handed down a collection of opinions in which they set forth their views of what the Christian life outlined in Scripture demanded; with respect to human sexuality this became total continence, if possible, and marriage for the sake of avoiding fornications in the incontinent. The Medievals then set out to detail the determinative moral principles relative to all venereal acts, in or out of marriage.

The medieval period's fullest and most important discussion of sexual sins was undertaken by Thomas Aquinas. His radical insistence on the absolute infallibility of scientific knowledge,[11] his dedication to reason, and his focus on the primacy of charity in theology could have brought him to a serious modification of Augustine's view. It did not.

Thomas was dedicated to the proposition that knowledge comes through the senses. Renowned for his own purity and as a successor to the Patristic heritage, Thomas took

Augustine as a theological teacher and developed his discussion of sexuality within an Augustinian universe of discourse. Despite his rational Aristotelian approach, he failed to overcome the limitations of the negative attitudes within which his efforts were confined; instead his talents were applied to a discussion of human sexuality in terms of its place in the scheme of things as part of the virtue of temperance. Thus in the *Summa Theologica* Thomas offers four articles on chastity, considering whether it is a virtue, whether it is a general virtue, whether it is distinct from abstinence, and whether purity belongs to it. He offers five articles on virginity, showing that it is a virtue, that it is more excellent than marriage, that it is lawful; he discusses what it consists in, and says that it is not the greatest of all virtues. But he offers no less than seventeen articles on lechery and its parts.[12]

Needless to say, Aquinas accepted the general orientation of tradition in the area of sexual morality. Included in this acceptance was the Pauline hierarchy of virtuous states (virginity, widowhood, marriage) and the implication that continence is virtue and incontinence is evil. Only the offsetting good of procreation is sufficient justification for escape from the heat of passion into the sacrament of matrimony.

The predictable result was the view that the legitimate use of human sexuality lay exclusively in valid sacramental marriage and that any other use was intemperate and evil. The biological obviousness of sexual reproduction only strengthened its heterosexual, sacramental, procreative orientation as the clear, straightforward, indisputable, and, as it ultimately came to be regarded, *natural* view of the true underlying reality in question. In effect this very *naturalness,* which was elaborated into the "natural law" doctrine on sexuality, placed the doctrine beyond debate and hence beyond reasoning.

The fundamental tie between coitus and procreation was normative for Thomas and lay behind his most basic assumption, namely, that *coitus should be natural.* He wrote that since procreation, unlike food and drink, is not a matter of individual need but of the need of the whole species, it is not necessary for all men to devote themselves to acts of generation. He further stated that intercourse is divinely instituted and consequently is not to be changed by man. Where discussion about coitus is concerned, therefore, there cannot be reasoned debate; rather the order of nature is to be distinguished in this matter from the order of reason.

Coitus was thus absolutized as part of the divinely instituted *ordo naturae.* Debate was precluded; the norm for coitus was what was "natural," that is, "conducive to the conservation of the species." In particular, coitus should be procreation-oriented; and for Thomas that meant marital (sacramental, heterosexual) and generative (inseminative, man above woman).[13]

Thomas did not consider touches and kisses in themselves mortally sinful; they become so only when they are lustful. Neither did he think nocturnal pollution sinful, unless induced by excessive eating or drinking, thinking lascivious thoughts during the day, or some other similar self-indulgence.

It is interesting to note that, despite the detailed consideration he gave to the sins of lechery, Thomas Aquinas took a tolerant attitude toward prostitution; he believed it to be a necessary evil without which great good would be lost or greater evil fostered. His justification was not based on a recognition of the futility of a civil-law prohibition, but rather represented consent to a male-centered, double-standard view on questions of sexual morality.

Aquinas, then, set the tone for theological speculation on sexuality for the next several centuries.[14] Augustine had synthesized Patristic thought on the subject; Thomas, fortified by the thought of both Aristotle and Augustine, put forth a powerful, detailed, highly rational presentation of the Church's position. Yet it was destined to be regarded as a moral analysis carried out in a discrete-act framework rather than an effort to understand the positive functions of sexuality in human life. In spite of this, however, his view was to be normative and his analysis was to be taken for granted by his successors.

To sum up, like the thought of the medieval period generally, Aquinas' position toward sexuality was greatly influenced by the attitudes of his time. There was persistence in considering abstractly the chaste states of life and in awarding to virginity the excellence of the "highest" state. The clerical model of celibacy reinforced the exaltation of virginity at the expense of marriage, which represented a condescension to the inability to remain continent, a submission to what was tainted with evil, and an obstacle to a "higher" life of divine service. Subtle distinction was present in the treatment of men and women, despite the Pauline insistence that all are one in Christ. The emphasis on virginity and widowhood was still an emphasis on female virtue, and the tolerance of prostitution implied an acceptance of a dual standard or at least assent to the idea that men cannot be expected to be as sexually continent as women.

The exaltation of virginity as a superideal was extended by praise of widowhood and celibacy; and the encouragement of vows of virginity among minors, and even between bride and groom, only heightened the negativism of the period toward marriage and, of course, toward the use of sex outside of marriage. The whole atmosphere was one which psychologically must have caused hopelessness in some, and loss of contact with reality in others. The effect on those who could not escape their sexual nature, no matter how hard they tried, must have been shattering.

## From Thomas Aquinas to Martin Le Maistre

The entire period from Thomas Aquinas (1225–1274) to Martin Le Maistre (1432–1481) was clearly one of continued interest in Aristotelianism. If Thomas had been controversial during his lifetime, he became only more so after his death which brought condemnation on the one hand and, on the other, his adoption by the Dominicans as official theologian. With his eventual canonization there came some broader special interest, but he was still not as influential as Duns Scotus (1266–1308) or William of Ockham (c.1280–c.1349) until the rise of the Jesuit order during the Counter Reformation. Then Thomism assumed great prominence; in fact the *Summa Theologica* replaced Peter Lombard's *Sentences* as the textbook of influence. It is noteworthy that Le Maistre's great attention to Thomas' thought was prompted by its Aristotelian framework.

It is in the writings of Le Maistre that the initial innovation with respect to the doctrine that grew out of the attitudes of Paul, Augustine, and Aquinas can be seen. Le Maistre accepted Paul's "virginity-widowhood-marriage" hierarchy of the states of chastity, but rejected the rule of Augustine that intercourse might be undertaken licitly in marriage only for the sake of procreation or the rendering of the debt. His importance as innovator lies in the fact that by rejecting the Augustinian rule, as he called it, he began the development of a separation of human sexuality as such, from human sexuality as procreative; and that development has in this century led to extremely significant reconsideration of the traditional sexual ethic. Le Maistre, although not a figure of particular importance in his own time, laid the foundations for the gradual changes that came about in the thought of more influential figures like Thomas Sanchez and Alphonsus Liguori; he is also the precursor of many contemporary Roman Catholic ethicists.

Le Maistre's methodology was to reanalyze the traditional discrete-act treatment of sexuality put forth by Thomas. He spoke of sexuality as something good in itself, as something not merely acceptable but valuable. As a secular priest, he may have been using the fruits of his experience with penitents as a guideline for his rejection of some of the traditional norms. Nevertheless, by breaking down the Augustinian rule and consequently loosening the tie between sexual activity and procreation, Le Maistre began to give human sexuality a value in itself. He thus began to weaken to some extent the notion of a necessary biological link between sexuality per se and sexuality as procreative.

The significance of Le Maistre's reevaluation of human sexuality as an entity apart from procreation is that it serves as the key to an understanding of the contemporary approach of Roman Catholic ethicists to problems in this area.

The commitment to the marital norm, which entirely dominated the traditional attitude toward sexuality, was (since procreation was understood to be the ordinary outcome of intercourse) an essential protection for the child who might be born of any sexual union. But even the marital norm itself would be altered by Le Maistre's extraordinary approach.

In a clearly rational, highly philosophical, and systematic fashion, Le Maistre pitted reason against tradition. If human sexuality was to be set forth as desirable in itself, then a necessary first step had to be a severance of the link between intercourse and procreation. By rejecting the Augustinian rule Le Maistre assumed that there can be other legitimate intentions in marital intercourse besides procreation. He held that an individual could engage in intercourse in order to avoid committing adultery. One could also seek intercourse in order to calm one's mind, for the sake of health, and even for the sake of pleasure. What is remarkable in all this is that these intentions are explicitly nonprocreative in character. Of particular interest is the fact that Le Maistre removed the element of sin from the motive of sexual pleasure which Augustine had characterized as evil.

Ultimately, Le Maistre even held that it was not heresy to maintain that simple fornication is not a mortal sin (provided that the individual has not determined in his own conscience that Scripture must be interpreted as forbidding simple fornication). The contemporary reader can thus see in Le Maistre, even though his influence was to be slight, a shift from the absolutism of Thomas' natural law doctrine. In other words, Le Maistre's use of reason as the tool of his analysis represented a fifteenth-century movement away from any "god" (such as nature) which fetters man's reason, and signals the imminent death of such a "god" in the history of innovation about sexuality.

## Thomas Sanchez and Alphonsus Liguori

Twenty-five years after Le Maistre's death the Church was deeply involved in the Reformation and Counter Reformation. It was a time in which there was great reluctance even to discuss sexual matters, hence there was no meaningful innovation or even attempted innovation along these lines, and the direction pointed out by Le Maistre was largely forgotten. Two writers are significant, however: Thomas Sanchez (1550–1610), because he wrote a book devoted exclusively to sexual questions; and Alphonsus Liguori (1697–1787), because he proved to be a figure of tremendous influence for the entire nineteenth century and, consequently, for the moral theologians whose manuals were popular in the first half of the twentieth century.

Sanchez, in 1602, published a book on marriage entitled *De Sancto Matrimonii Sacramento,* which established his reputation as the principal authority of his era on the subject of marriage and human sexuality. In the work he presented a casuistic approach which was intended to help the priest in the confessional deal with matters of sexual morality. Like more general works of the period, the book was a product of the attempt on the part of the principally Jesuit moralists of the post-Tridentine era to make ethics more precise.

Sanchez set forth the rather enlightened position that an ordinary married couple in the state of grace need not concern themselves with intentions when having intercourse.

He found no sin in spouses who intended only to copulate as spouses. On the basis of his contention that such a couple automatically have a requisite good intention, he refuted the Augustinian rule just as Le Maistre did. He applied a commonsense confessional norm, as Le Maistre may have been doing, and thereby brought ethical considerations into greater harmony with ordinary Christian morality.

Sanchez took a rather remarkable position on orgasm outside licit marital intercourse. He deemed such a voluntary ejaculation to be strictly forbidden, even to save one's life. His reason diverged radically from the overall procreation-orientation of the tradition: It is liable to be abused, since an individual might seek the pleasure of such ejaculation as his "sovereign good." It is an interesting hypothesis, although clearly an unlikely one. For man does not live by ejaculation alone. The thirst for air is much more compelling than the thirst for sexual satisfaction. Therefore if there is danger in seeking anything as one's sovereign good, then the desire for the very breath of life might, by this reasoning, represent peril. What is most striking about Sanchez' analysis, however, is his conclusion that what is immoral in nonmarital orgasm is the risk of abuse. For that conclusion yields the insight that what this prohibition protects is an apparently deep-seated notion that human beings—much like children—need to be shielded from the freedom to make decisions about sexual morality on account of their weakness with respect to this area of human life.

Sanchez also took an interesting position concerning a woman who has been raped. He maintained that she could try to expel the semen of her attacker before generation occurs, for her act is one of self-defense against an unjust aggressor. A diametrically opposite view was taken by the key figure of the eighteenth century, Alphonsus Liguori. He disagreed with Sanchez on the question of expulsion of the seed after insemination has occurred, for he refused to separate insemination and generation on the grounds that even in the case of rape the seed was ordered to generation. He was thus ultimately forced to separate generation and education with this doctrine.

On motives for seeking intercourse, Liguori saw Paul's teaching as clearly indicating that an individual might undertake it without sin for the sake of avoiding adultery. He held that in this instance intercourse was licit, even though the individual might have a positive hope that procreation would not follow.

## The Final Rule:
## Thomas Aquinas' Natural Law Doctrine

It was from such a background as this, then, that the Roman Catholic doctrine of sexual ethics, to which the present generation is heir, developed. As already indicated, Thomas Aquinas became the guiding light of the Catholic Church's study of rational philosophy and theology. And it was Thomas' formulation of the doctrine of natural law in the area of sexual morality which became the basis for determining the morality of acts of a sexual nature.

As we have seen, Thomas' most fundamental assumption was that coitus should be natural. He further argued that the morality of all sexual acts must be determined by their conformity to "the natural." But "natural," as Thomas defined it, was in fact quite arbitrary. This, which shall be discussed in fuller detail later, was the weakness of the natural law doctrine. It could survive only if the natural could be demonstratively shown to be a fixed, clear, indisputable norm.

Thomas' approach to the natural law doctrine[15] is presented most clearly in his *Summa Theologica,* II-II, Question 154. In the second article he responds to an objection that had been made to his contention that simple fornication is a mortal sin. Every mortal sin, the opposition had argued, is contrary to charity—that is, it is injurious to either God or neighbor. But simple fornication injures neither. Therefore it is not a mortal sin. Thomas grants that the conditions of mortal sin have been validly stated; what has been overlooked is the fact that simple fornication, because it is opposed to the good of the child to be born of the union, *is* contrary to the love of neighbor. Thomas here is following the view he presents in the body of the article, where he indicates that simple fornification is a mortal sin because it implies an inordinateness which directly and adversely affects a human life, specificially the life of the potential offspring who needs the care of both mother and father. Such care demands that a particular man be united to a particular woman, and that they remain together for a long period of time in order to properly rear the child.

In Article 12 of the same question Thomas faces the objection that the so-called sins against nature—heterosexual anal intercourse, masturbation, homosexuality, bestiality, or the like—injure neither God nor neighbor. He asserts that, on the contrary, in sins against nature the injury is precisely an injury to God. This is so because the order of nature is violated, and this order comes from God.

The weak link in this kind of reasoning is, of course, to be found in the rather circular argumentation: The sin against nature injures God because it violates the order of nature that comes from God. This is tantamount to saying that any sin that an individual or a group decides is against nature is therefore a sin against God because God is the author of nature. But, as mentioned previously, the decision as to what is against nature is a rather arbitrary one. Concepts of "the natural" have changed drastically. Once thought to be static, fixed, firm, and determined, "the natural" is now regarded as not only not static, not fixed, not firm, not determined, not final, but—as far as man is concerned—nonexistent. The reason for this is that it is part of man's very nature to be able to alter "the natural" as he finds it in the universe. And for this same reason Thomas' doctrine is vulnerable to serious criticism.

In Thomas' natural law doctrine there is an assumption

that natural coitus should not be altered by man because it was instituted by God. This means that God has ordained an order of nature that Thomas contrasts with the order of reason. It is ironic that, by so contrasting the orders of nature and reason, Thomas points up the weakness of his doctrine, for when it is examined in the light of reason, that doctrine is destroyed.

Recall, for example, the previously discussed objection concerning sins against nature: Fornication may be sinful because the potential offspring would have no definitive parentage; but what of anal intercourse, masturbation, homosexuality, bestiality, and so forth? Since they injure neither a living person nor a yet unborn one, where is the evil in these acts? Thomas' response is really an acknowledgment that, although reason tells us that there would be no one injured in any of these instances, nevertheless because there is an order of nature set up by God which dictates the natural mode of intercourse, it is (again) God who is injured by these and other sins against nature.

This kind of thinking elaborates a givenness with respect to man's sexual acts that does violence to man's freedom to use his reason. The givenness, moreover, asserts that what makes sexual activity proper and natural is the biological integrity of the act of insemination to which Thomas assigns the absolute value of God. In short, despite man's special gift of reason, this one particular aspect of animal behavior is taken as normative for man—that is, dumb animals, possessing no reason, did not appear to Thomas to violate the integrity of the act of insemination. The biological link between sexual intercourse and procreation, which makes procreation dependent on intercourse, is turned around to make intercourse intentionally dependent upon its procreative purpose. This biological function of the sex act is then taken as an unalterable given from God, and other uses of sexuality are called unnatural.

What Thomas means by natural, then, is clearly that

the semen must be deposited in the vagina, that insemination has an absolute value to it. Again the basis for establishing this absolute value and for assigning to insemination the absolute value of God comes directly from the possible biological orientation of sexual intercourse to procreation. Specifically, then, the gravity of sexual offenses derives from the injury done to what is seen as the welfare of the species, for sexuality is taken to be ordered to the preservation of the species. While Thomas had in mind the welfare of the unborn child in the case of fornication, he was, where sins against nature were concerned, thinking of the good of the conservation of the species, to which he assigned a value equivalent to divinity.

To repeat, the natural law doctrine of Aquinas hardened into the rule that has remained the guiding force in theology right up to the present time, if Pope Paul's recent encyclical *Humanae Vitae* is to be taken as an indication of the attitude of the official institutional Church. This doctrine consequently had a decided effect on those who were subjected to it in their religious lives, particularly in relation to their visits to the confessional. Certainly the doctrine was broad enough in scope to cover every conceivable sexual act and to provide the basis for a rigorous determination of the morality of each. Thus in the present century, for example, Pope Pius XI in his *Casti Conubii,* discussing the nature and dignity of Christian marriage, held that the conjugal act is destined primarily by nature for the begetting of children. He therefore concluded that those who deliberately frustrate this natural power and purpose sin against nature and the law of God, and commit an act that is intrinsically vicious. In addition, any directly venereal use of sexuality outside of marriage is strictly forbidden.

The Church's general teaching, then, was still tied to the notion that sexuality was ordained to procreation and as such could be used only by the married. As a result, there are basically two areas of concern in the present century:

one, the area of marriage; and the other, the area of sexuality outside of marriage. These areas each have an essentially different history, although the ethical treatment of both is tending to converge at present. In the case of the use of sexuality within marriage, the 1920's, 30's, and 40's saw the emerging strength of the advocates of birth control, as well as an insistence—at first by all Christian Churches and later by the Roman Catholic Church alone—that to practice contraception was to violate nature and, consequently, to sin. The confinement of the use of sexuality to marriage, on the other hand, was a strict view, but nevertheless strongly supported in the overall Christian tradition.

One source of the strict attitude of the Catholic Church toward the use of sexuality may have been the fact that professional celibates had developed the sexual ethic. No matter how well intentioned, they certainly had to be influenced by an attitude toward sexuality engendered by the very ideal to which they themselves were committed. They saw their ideal of the Christian life of asceticism, sacrifice, love, and the imitation of Christ as including denial of the use of sexuality, and failed to see the same possibility in radical affirmation of its use. This was not particularly unusual in view of the traditional flesh-spirit conflict which regarded the use of sex as highly suspect, and even evil. As we have seen, Augustine certainly regarded it in this light, though he felt that the purposes of procreation and the rendering of the debt somehow moderated the evil or compensated for it. The result was that the possibility of a unique theology of sex for the layman was precluded.

The difficulty with the attempt to translate the model for clerical celibacy into the model for marriage was that it failed to recognize the uniqueness and function of marriage as a way of existential commitment having as its very essence the radical affirmation of the other as person, which in God's plan is beautifully and preeminently effected by means of sexual union. There was a distortion of lay spirituality introduced by those clerics who attempted to make "partial abstinence" the lay model of sexual life.

The consequence of the doctrine, then, as it hardened and persisted well into the 1950's and 60's, was the production of the kinds of moral theology manuals, discussed in the first part of this book, which dealt with sins of the flesh in extensive detail as objectively serious. The view of these authors was that directly venereal sexuality had no place whatsoever in the life of a human being who was not married. In marriage such actions were to be oriented basically toward procreation. As a result of this kind of theology, sins of the flesh became the central religious problem in the lives of an alarmingly large number of Roman Catholics. The Catholic adolescent, for example, has traditionally found the matter of impurity a stumbling block to the peace of a clear conscience and joyful participation in the sacraments. For many individuals, the trying period of adolescence was followed by an adulthood that also was marred by this one insuperable obstacle to spiritual peace.

Even among the married, many have deprived themselves of the sacraments for years because their feeling of guilt over numerous failures to be "pure" has left them with a deep sense of unworthiness and shame. Others have neglected to root out of their lives habits of contentiousness, anger, and lying because their energies have been directed at the only sin which, according to traditionalist theologians, admits of no light matter but rather is always objectively serious, having as it does an intrinsic moral valuation of a negative character (evil). Such for the Catholic was the burden of being flesh.

What is more significant still, however, is that it was the burden of an inadequate world view. Until the present, man—despite the infinite potentiality of his reason—has seen himself as just another static "given" among the other creatures of that "natural" order of things by which he—

creatively evolutionary being, rational free spirit, participator in the divine—was oppressed. It was that world view, currently being rent asunder by the pace of contemporary experience, which lay behind man's inhumanity toward himself.

## Footnotes 2

1. Heribert Jone, *Moral Theology,* rev. ed. (Westminister, Md.: The Newman Press, 1963).

2. "Lightness of matter" is a reference to the possibility that certain acts and species of acts are not so intrinsically serious as to constitute mortal sin, a complete turning away from God. To hold that sexual sins admit no lightness of matter is to assert that they are always, objectively speaking, seriously sinful.

3. H. Noldin, *Summa Theologiae Moralis* (New York: F. Pustet, 1936), sec. 3, p. 58.

4. Arthur Vermeersch, *De Castitate et de vitiis contrariis* (Rome: Gregorian University Press, 1921), p. 301.

5. Bernard Häring, *The Law of Christ* (Westminster, Md.: The Newman Press, 1963), pp. 350-352.

6. For example, besides ordinary celibacy or virginity, the encouragement of "spiritual marriages"—that is, marriage without sexual acts—and the encouragement of widows and widowers not to remarry.

7. The warnings to virgins not to participate in marriage celebrations, for example.

8. Considerable debate raged over Saint Paul's words in I Cor. 7:15: "But if the unbelieving depart, let him depart. A brother or a sister is not under bondage in such cases; rather God hath called us to peace." Ambrosiaster had suggested the commentary on the text that would allow divorce and remarriage of the converted partner in a pagan marriage should his or her spouse refuse to live in peace. The debate thus focused on whether or not pagan marriages were indissoluble and, if so, what special circumstances of conversion might render them dissoluble.

9. Hildebrand, dedicated to the Church's temporal as well as spiritual power, in his program of ascetic reformation and renewal ordered priests to separate from their wives and concubines, and not to marry.

10. Paul had taught explicitly in I Cor. 6:16 that it was by coitus that man and woman became one flesh, the sign of true supernatural marriage. Yet the Medievals, under Patristic influence, hesitated to vest in "incontinence" the essential element of valid marriage. Moreover, Augustine saw the virginal marriage of

Joseph and Mary as valid on account of their mutual donation alone, which entailed no expression in intercourse. Cf. Augustine's *On Marriage and Concupiscence* 1.12.

11. Thomas Aquinas, because of his utter confidence in the total and absolute validity of science and reason, makes them independent of faith and ecclesiastical authority. He thus effectively separates philosophy and theology by insisting upon their methodic difference, and at the same time unites the two on the grounds of their total noncontradictory validity.

12. Thomas lists the species as the vice against nature, simple fornication, incest, adultery, seduction, and rape.

13. It is interesting to speculate whether the norm for coitus would become contraceptive if "the conservation of the species" were to be better served by nonprocreation.

14. *The Code of Canon Law,* Canon 1366, sec. 2, declares: "In the study of rational philosophy and theology, and in the instruction of students, the professor should follow entirely the method, doctrine, and principles of the Angelic Doctor, and hold them religiously." Pope Pius XI, in his encyclical *Studiorum Ducem,* published on June 29, 1923, urged that this Canon be regarded as a sacred command.

15. The reader is reminded that I am using the expression "natural law doctrine" to refer to that particular interpretation and application of natural law theory which became the accepted ground of sexual ethics within Roman Catholicism.

# 3
# PROTEST, CONFLICT, AND REVISION

Ethics differs from faith in that ethics is subject to reason whereas faith takes us beyond the rational. There is a tendency in certain religious groups not to question ethical prescriptions but rather to divinize them, to supernaturalize them, to place them beyond debate, beyond question, beyond reason. The natural law doctrine might well have been called the supernatural law doctrine precisely because the effort to establish it as the general rule for the determination of the morality of sexual acts really succeeded in divinizing, or supernaturalizing, the rule.

The tradition has always subscribed to the idea that procreation is good. What has crept into the tradition is the false notion that procreation is an *absolute* good. It has often been forgotten that the tradition really links procreation and the proper rearing of offspring as one goal, so that procreation apart from the notion of proper rearing is not in and of itself a goal. Nevertheless, the theory that life under any circumstances is better than no life at all hypothesizes that it is better to populate the kingdom of heaven with an additional soul no matter what the earthly life circumstances of that soul may have been.

Pressure to change the natural law doctrine of human sexuality first emerged within a limited context. It was a pressure to control birth. How might a married couple have intercourse without having to concern themselves with possible conception? The question was not a new one. Couples having intercourse have probably asked themselves this same question for hundreds of years.

The sharp decline in the birth rate in France during the first half of the nineteenth century was the result of a widespread desire on the part of the French to regulate the number of children born. What distinguished the modern situation was its international aspect, specifically the universal concern for the way in which the population explosion was threatening the quality of life in many parts of the world. In a world overburdened by people, with millions of children without parents, without a home, without proper upbringing, it was even suggested that married couples desirous of being parents should adopt children in need of a home rather than have their own. Genuine parenthood, at least ideal parenthood, is not physical or biological; it is instead a relationship established, not by biological accident, but by deliberate existential commitment. Actually, the value in physically producing offspring is that they tend to look like the parents. And yet this may be a disadvantage; for it helps perpetuate the idea that children are or ought to be carbon copies of their parents, a myth that has often caused great hardship and difficulty in families where children were expected to be not only physical but psychological doubles of father or mother.

There are probably few couples, however, who wish to practice birth control because they see their possible reproduction as threatening the stability of world population, and widespread interest in birth control stemmed principally from crises of a family nature.

As advanced technology gave rise to increased mobility among families, a general movement from agrarian to urban living, and an alteration in the status of women, it also produced a quite drastic change in the quality of human life in the advanced countries of the world. Many educated individuals viewed further procreation as a threat to personal health, to family stability, or to their ability to properly educate the children for whom they were responsible.

The context, then, was one in which a great number of people wished to avoid the possibility of having children. Among these were the married couples who felt that they had a right to intercourse, but who did not wish to practice abstinence. Yet, though the Lambeth Conference of 1930 was willing to allow Anglo-Catholics to use other methods apart from complete abstinence as a means of birth control, Roman Catholics received no such permission. According to the teaching of the organized Church, couples had to choose between childbearing and continence; there was no third alternative.

In 1951, however, there was a radical change made in the teaching. Pope Pius XII in October of that year delivered his *Allocution to Midwives,* and in the address he indicated his acceptance of the calculation of a woman's sterile period as a legitimate approach to birth regulation.

Prior to the pope's recognition of the rhythm method as licit, the idea that a presumably fertile couple might engage in sexual union with the deliberate intention of avoiding pregnancy was unheard of. Such intent stood in direct opposition to the rule of Augustine, to the view of Thomas Aquinas, and to the traditional fundamental assumption that procreation is the end upon which coitus depends for its justification. The pope's acceptance of the use of rhythm was therefore the most momentous of all decisions in the modern history of innovation in Roman Catholic sexual ethics. It was a crucial blow dealt to an otherwise relatively untouched structure.

Intercourse had been permitted among the aged and other married couples who knew that they could not expect to procreate for reasons completely beyond their control. And to that extent the traditional doctrine was already weak. But the 1951 papal statement was of special significance because, first, it emanated from the highest authority in the Church; and secondly—speaking as it did to couples who might expect procreation to be the ordinary result of their intercourse—it deviated from the traditional teaching that intercourse had to be, at least in intention, open to such procreation.

The pope's pronouncement had extremely important implications for the theological development of revisionist thinking, for it implied that intercourse and procreation are not bound together by anything more significant than sheer biology unregulated by man's reasoning power. The intercourse-procreation link, which had made intercourse intentionally dependent upon procreation because procreation was considered biologically dependent upon intercourse, was broken. Gone was the idea that procreation is an absolute duty to which those having intercourse are obliged. Implicit as well was papal recognition and acceptance of the idea that intercourse had purposes and values apart from any possibility of procreation. With an inadequately developed biology thus removed from its role as ethics-teacher, the way was paved for rejection of the barrier to reasoning implicit in the so-called natural law doctrine which had functioned in Roman Catholicism as an absolute norm of sexual ethics.

The natural law doctrine had required that all ethical judgments about each and every use of human sexuality be made on the basis of whether or not the individual sexual act followed the form deemed suitable for procreation and the proper rearing of offspring. That form was, of course, heterosexual and inseminative. The doctrine, as has been pointed out previously, was elaborated to a point where it was rendered as absolute and imperious a law of nature as that of gravity. The whole concept of natural law, instead of being the product of considerations based upon reasonable choices, placed upon individuals burdens that, in the present period at least, appeared to be irrational. The revisionists felt that only a new understanding of nature could rectify such a misconception and open up the possibility that the guidelines for the protection of human life might be altered to meet the interpersonal needs of the sexual relationship and the suprapersonal needs of the world in the crisis induced by population expansion. With the emphasis shifted to personal responsibility and personal freedom, it followed—in the light of the theological implication of the pope's acceptance of the rhythm method—that a number of contraceptive methods could not be objectively classified as immoral. The decision whether or not to procreate belonged to the individuals having intercourse.

The value of responsible parenthood was now accorded the importance it really deserved. Though the Church's strong tradition had insisted upon the combined goals of procreation and the proper rearing of children as an end toward which the sacrament of matrimony was directed, emphasis had shifted to the goal of procreation, so that the proper rearing of offspring was largely ignored. Revisionist thinking, on the contrary, was a call to responsible parenthood. Undue emphasis on the mere ability to procreate was ended. The sacredness imputed to sex was no longer to be allowed to encourage procreative sexual activity apart from very pertinent rational considerations about the provisions necessary for proper rearing of the child.

The reinterpretation of natural law doctrine, substituting reason for biology, meant that the subject would always be open to revision on the basis of new reasoning. This openness to revision led to the conclusion that no distinction could be made between methods of contraception such as the use of the condom (mechanical withholding of the sperm) and the use of the pill (chemical withholding of the ovum). The revision also led to the collapse of much of the remaining ethical structure built up in Roman Catholicism with respect to the ethics of human sexuality. The dissolution of the contraception regulation introduced considerations about the separation of human sexuality in itself from human sexuality as procreative. Such dissolution similarly dissolved a number of other ties which bound together the ethical structure of the Roman Catholic view of sexuality.

The heated controversy over birth control began in earnest with the publication of *The Time Has Come,* by John Rock. Rock, a prominent physician and a Roman Catholic, characterized the crisis over birth control as the first world crisis in history. As a scientist, his concern stemmed from the population explosion and his own theological appreciation of the possibilities raised by the production of the progesterone pill. Rock, though not a theologian, understood the theological problem. He saw the religious conflict over birth control as a conflict over methods rather than objectives. He felt that a doctrine of responsible parenthood was emerging in Roman Catholicism. (It had been there all along, to be sure, but had been badly neglected.)

Dr. Rock also felt that a new light was being cast on the doctrine of natural law. And this was indeed the case, since all those who had been looking for a revision of the rules of sexual ethics that would be based ultimately upon the natural law doctrine were finally beginning to realize that it was part of their vocation to frustrate "nature"— understood narrowly in an older world view—by plumbing the depths of that "nature" as understood in the new world view. For indeed it was truly the "nature" of man, as a free rational being in the process of determining his own evolution, to escape from the oppression of a sterile world of static order dictated by accident, and to create his own world; and even to destroy and re-create it, if need be.

70

Clearly this kind of thinking is behind the writing of all of the revisionists, as they have been called here, who suggested any movement away from the old rules. Their assertions include the following: (1) the rationale for the natural law doctrine as presented by Roman Catholic moralists had never provided clear, persuasive, and conclusive arguments for the doctrine; (2) reason would incline certain couples to want in conscience to practice birth control; (3) Catholics alone could hardly be privy to the natural law doctrine if it were really a question of natural law based on reason and not on authority; (4) ethical formulation must necessarily be mutable; (5) married couples are not chained by lust; (6) the use of sexuality is important in strengthening and expressing the union of two people in love; (7) an animal's need for any *one* of the several specific purposes of an action will initiate the action, while the other effects—if not needed—will be inhibited in some way; life would be impossible without this type of control; (8) the purpose of childbearing is the ultimate formation of the child as a fully reared adult, not as a newborn babe; (9) magisterial pronouncements must be understood within the context of the society out of which they emanated; (10) the doctrine of the primary end of marriage would be considerably more applicable to a society devastated by periodic plagues than to a society like our own; (11) it is necessary, in seeking criteria for defining the nature of the material act, to avoid taking a merely biological or a merely legal point of view; (12) sexual intercourse, not merely a discrete physical act, reaches out into the total texture of man's life; and (13) some who would use contraceptives may love each other more than some who did not use them. All these assertions uniformly point away from oppression of man by "natural law" toward a new view of him as a creative participant in nature's evolution.

Much of the pressure on the doctrine seemed to emanate from a concern for the value of interpersonal love.

For the first time in the history of the tradition, the value of interpersonal love was held out as a valid motive, not merely for marrying or for having intercourse, but for deliberately frustrating that particular biological function which had always been regarded as coitus' "natural purpose." Love was coming into its own at last.

Yet love is so terribly misunderstood, so frighteningly distorted by patterns of socialization. All of us want to love and to be loved. We need to be needed because we have so much love to give. This is more than a learned response. When the mother teaches love to her infant, she is really creating a life-style for the child. And the creation of life-style leads to the establishment of a world view through the inculcation of an existential attitude toward all that is.

The human child cannot survive without care. However poor that care may be, it must reach a certain minimal level. The mother's care of the child both in the womb and after birth, if it is adequate for the child's survival, is a principal factor in setting the tone for his understanding of his nature, his needs, and his life in the world. Although we cannot for a moment underestimate the validity of the learned response of the child and the extent to which the environment influences him, we are dealing here with part of the very substratum of human nature. In these roots one can see the ethical message of Christianity as well as the ethical message of a number of other great religions of the world.

The Christian ethical message of love of neighbor, like the more popular Golden Rule, teaches that each individual needs to recognize the likeness of his own feelings in those of his fellowmen. Except in those circumstances in which psychopathology has interrupted psychological growth, all men share by nature a common disposition of goodwill toward their fellowmen which Adler called social interest. The point of Christ's ethical imperative is aimed at overcoming the negative trait of intolerance. Christ uncompromisingly demands that intolerance be excluded from every existential situation. One man rejects, condemns, hates, or mistreats another human soul. That is sin. And that is why the law of Christ is a law of genuine love of one's fellowman. Love *is* the answer.

Yet some men will use any excuse, even a supposedly religious one, to set themselves above their fellowmen. For centuries it has been part of normal human existence for the majority to consider themselves superior to the minority. Whites have lorded it over blacks, Christians over Jews, heterosexuals over homosexuals, the sane over the insane; the list is endless. All these examples share the madness to which one subscribes if he makes rigid value judgments predicated upon an inherent, fundamental inequality among men which is supposedly manifested by their falling into categories such as "majority" and "minority." Prejudice, in fact, is the modern counterpart of the feud. What is remarkable is that those who scorn the notion of feud are often engaging in one. They are perpetuating the same prejudices of their forebears—without reason, without common sense.

The natural law doctrine of sexuality is an example of such prejudice because it is simply the interpretation by one man and his followers of what is natural, and it has been upheld by a tyrannical authority attempting to preserve itself by retaining a vague "order" which a majority often demands because they see that "order" (the status quo) as sacred. Other men might see the issue in an entirely different light; therefore, it is unforgivable to deify the majority opinion and thereby delude others or dominate them by fear aroused by what is in reality a prejudice. Where is love? Where are tolerance, understanding, and Christianity?

For example, is it intrinsically wrong to masturbate because masturbation frustrates a possible goal of nature? If it is, then how can it be right to air-condition a room, plow a field, cut one's hair, transplant a kidney, give or take a blood transfusion, dam a river, or prolong life with chemicals and other devices? Masturbation seems neither less "natural" nor more harmful than cigarette smoking; yet people inhale cigarettes with one breath and defend the natural law doctrine with the next.

Concomitant with the general attack upon the natural law doctrine has been an emphasis on the broader role of sexuality in human life. The historically narrow view found in the writings of the Roman Catholic theologians has been expanded to include a deeper appreciation of the role of sexuality in human life, and its function is seen as going far beyond the bounds of isolated, discrete actions. Most of the work in this area revolves around the psychological contributions of men whose personalist orientation stands in direct contrast to the objective legalistic orientation of the traditional Roman Catholic sexual ethic.

One of the principal contributions of modern psychology has been to confirm that mental illness has its roots in the breakdown of human relationships on the level of the love, care, and concern that men must have for one another. No matter what psychological school of thought one follows, one is led to the inescapable conclusion that it is really on this level that difficulties occur. When relationships between people break down, then people break down. The reason is that being human, modern existentialist theory tells us, means to be constituted by one's relationships to others. And in all relationships man participates as a sexual being.

Sexuality has been of primary importance in the development of psychoanalysis largely because Freud himself developed a very strong sexually-oriented theory. In Freud's view man's basic anxiety stems from sexual repression; the disturbed individual's difficulty is that he compartmentalizes sexuality and represses some facet of it, instead of mastering its developmental phases. Other psychologists take a more expanded approach. While including sexuality, they put equal emphasis on broader dimensions of interpersonal experience. The renowned psychologist and author, Erich Fromm, for example, sees the problem of anxiety as essentially one of separateness. A basic need of man is the need to escape separateness, to feel close to another person.

Another prominent psychologist and author, Erik Erikson, also sees man's anxieties in interpersonal terms resulting from inadequate social responses along a developmental timetable. For Erikson, however, failure to work through any developmental state in a "normal" way does not necessarily produce an irrevocably "abnormal" individual. Corrective relationship experiences during adolescence may provide opportunities to modify the anxieties brought about by earlier conflicts. Adler underscores Fromm's and Erikson's approaches by stressing the significance of interpersonal experiences in promoting or retarding emotional growth. He sees man's significance consisting of the satisfaction he experiences from contributing to the lives of others and having others contribute to his. Anxiety is the consequence of self-centered living. The way to combat it is by a return to concern and love.

But who dares to love? Who can face the prospect of loving truly? Love demands honesty; and honesty requires freedom. A process of humanization ought to set man free. It ought to maximize his infinite potential. Yet society rewards the unfree person. It rewards conformity, the very antithesis of free and creative response. Man's world alienates the individual from his deepest identity as human being by forcing him to play roles that have been heteronomously created by consensus and rationalization rather than by free personal choice and rational argument; they have been passed on, even genetically perhaps, in the archetypes of the collective unconscious. Conditioned to fear, men seem to prefer to delude themselves with the untruth rather than to live an unbounded free existence. If what is feared is indeed the meaninglessness of human life, then a genuine religious question is at issue. For when any group subscribes to a world view that destroys personal identity as part of its process of socialization, there is clear indication of that group's inability or unwillingness to distinguish between what human life really is and what it is not. In the case of sexuality, the natural law doctrine—a rationality-defying assumption that man is to follow a natural law much as animals do—serves to shield men from the difficult requirements of a truly free existence.

True love, then, cannot survive the enforced repression of the acting out of feelings, desires, and emotions of the true self. The true humanity of the individual, if it is pent up within, cannot benefit from the experience of living. The individual thus remains an uneducated child, untried, undeveloped. Existentially speaking, he dies from disuse. Could he but release himself, he might be free to love. He might overcome fear and dread. For love is healing. In fact, it is uniquely the acceptance which love radiates that is the antidote to the intolerance that produces alienation.

But who can face this? Who can begin truly to love? Only one who can see and understand his own estrangement from his very humanity. Only one who reaches the point where he is unable to go on playing the game of repressing his true feelings in order to fill the role expected of him. One must ultimately assume his true identity, that of a free, human, loving, creative being. One must be honest; one must love. If he is rebuffed and slaughtered, it does not matter. For he is free and has only discovered the lack of ability in another to respond humanly. It is the other's bad programming that is reprehensible. It is the other's recapitulative limit, his inability to meet each new encounter with total freedom and openness that is unfortunate. Those properly programmed as human should welcome love, should be able to accept it, to meet it with joy, and to return it. They should be anxious to give it in understanding and assistance. For love exists fully only when it is given and received.

In seeking another, one might indeed find emptiness, weakness. But if one can bring true love, genuine openness, and not recapitulation, to every encounter, then perhaps love will respond to love and a new creation may be brought into existence.

Love is the most fundamental element in any moral system. This is true of the Christian as well as other systems of ethics generally. Today we are witnessing modern youth's "new morality." It is a morality that says, "Make love, not war." Many people do not understand fully the profound implications of those four words. Love is creative, healing, supportive, and vivifying; whereas hatred and war are evils that tend to destroy persons and relationships, and to disintegrate the individual. When young people stand up in the name of the new morality and insist that we make love, not war, they are reminding us of this most fundamental moral presupposition. This is not to say that it is not a functional presupposition as well. Indeed, it is an affirmation of, among others, Fromm's theory, which offers love as the alternative to anxiety. Yet it is principally a moral commitment that is being urged upon us by the expression, "Make love"—an expression which customarily has referred specifically to the sexual act of love-making.

The mere fact that young people use this terminology and use it in this particular way is significant, for in the English-speaking world there is a taboo against speaking of making love. To bring sexuality out in the open in this fashion is something new. But what young people are saying in terms of the new morality, and specifically in terms of expressions like "Make love, not war," is that these two concepts are irreconcilable. It is war that is evil, not love-making. It is war that is lustful, not love of neighbor. It is making war that is psychopathic, not making love. To this extent young people are drawing attention to the hypocrisy of a society such as ours in which, until the present at least, to speak of love-making could be regarded as obscene while incalculable physical, financial, and emotional resources could be expended on weapons of hatred and destruction. Sexual love-making, although it is the subject matter of the "Song of Songs" in the Bible, was not a proper or fitting subject matter for families or children; but war, killing, death, and destruction were regarded as perfectly all right for young people to see in films and on television.

Modern youth is telling us that it is war that is obscene. If one wants to see all that is destructive in human life, all that is evil, then one need look only to war and hatred and man's inhumanity to his fellowman. Sexuality is not evil, although men have tended to emphasize the exclusively reproductive aspects of sexuality at the expense of its broader role in human life. There are indeed difficulties connected with sexuality, particularly when it is reproductive. There are possible social evils to which consideration should be given, and there exist frequent opportunities for moral evil as well. But one should not, out of the desire to check such evils, push uninformedly toward a denial of the vital developmental role of sexuality in human life.

Apart from the purely biological, there is a normative role for man's sexual potential in his development and fulfillment as human person. Sexuality serves a tremendously important function in this development precisely because in man, as in no other animal, the whole of the individual's being-toward-the-world is colored specifically by his being male or female. In other words, an individual's development relies upon his sexual category. Every child, in order to grow into an authentic human being, must develop as male or female. This is not to force a stereotype of maleness or femaleness on any individual. It is merely to say that the child, in order to develop normally into a fully human adult, must develop without ambiguity in regard to his being a sexed individual.

We are familiar with stereotypes—on the one hand of the totally masculine individual; on the other, of the totally feminine. To encounter either the total male or the total female would probably be unbearable. The total male would be so crude and primitive as to be unacceptable to most of us. The total female, on the other hand, would be so passive that she would offer little or nothing in response to human interests. Fortunately the total male and the total female are equally rare. All of us, instead, are a combination of male and female characteristics. Although the combination is sometimes unacceptable, it is usually satisfactory. It is true that there are those whose psychic makeup is so totally out of harmony with their physical makeup that their existence is very uncomfortable. Yet, although anomalies— either physical or mental—do occur in human life, and although these represent every conceivable combination, most individuals are fortunate enough to have one dominant orientation which falls into line with the physical qualities that are theirs by inheritance.

In general, sexuality plays a vital role in the individual's development to maturity through a process of growing self-awareness and a successful adjustment to one's sexuality. This ability to come to terms with one's maleness or femaleness is a basic requisite for being able to live comfortably in society. For, as the black man finds it impossible to discard color in an effort to integrate himself into society, so too would the individual find it impossible to discard his sexuality in his attempt to integrate himself as a loving, thinking, feeling person. In a word, to be a human being is to be sexual.

Most persons see sexual differentiation largely in terms of an emphasis on certain trivial and unimportant differences between man and woman. They miss the real significance of sexuality in human life. Physical differences seen as the source of sexual pleasure (the basis for so much advertising) are not really of importance. What is important is that an individual understand what it means to be sexed. Whether one is male or female is not critical, but rather that one is a sexed being. Thus the merely biological distinction between male and female is not at issue. The human race has, for example, more than adequately procreated without sex education courses. The goal of procreation is achievable totally apart from any insight into what it means to live a whole life as a sexed being, to build a human life with another person on the basis of a relationship that is sexual, and to be able to relate to all other persons on a genuinely personal and, hence, sexual level.

It is amazing that in a society that places such great emphasis on sex in its least important aspects one encounters so frequently the individual who has been brought up by parents who have tried to shield the child from his sexuality and have thereby impaired his recognition and mastery of it. Fierce battles are waged over sex education in schools, although trying to shroud the fact of a child's sexuality makes as little sense as trying to shroud the fact that he needs food to live. Some parents never achieve an adult-to-adult relationship with their offspring because of sex; it seems to block the mutual exchange of any genuine or meaningful communication of feeling or appreciation. Part of the reason for this failure in the parent-child relationship is that the parents—unable to adapt to the basic fact of the child's capacity for passionate sexual indulgence—refuse to recognize the free, independent adult-in-the-making on account of their own inability to come to guiltless terms with the reality and beauty of being a sexed animal.

Much of the difficulty obviously grew out of the traditional attitudes towards the sexual act as a mainly isolated function best reserved to its procreative purpose within the legitimizing confines of marriage. The theology of sexuality was stunted in its growth and limited to a highly biological analysis. Totally neglected was that other side of man's potential in which sexuality is closely linked to psychological development as a person and, through this development, to man's life of love in the world.

It was in this theological climate, then, that the revisionists began their movement. It was spurred on, beyond the impetus of Pius XII's acceptance of rhythm, by personalist insights from modern psychology. Those who had been moved to reflect upon the ethics of contraception out of concern for the inadequacies of rhythm, now directed the results of their speculations to the method itself. It seemed to them irrational to consider rhythm as the mode of contraception most in harmony with man's inventive nature. Aside from the fact that it did not work for many couples, it was highly artificial, humiliating, and dehumanizing—natural only in the most animalistic sense. In their opinion rhythm reduced the problem of contraception to a supremely non-rational, mechanistic, biological level, and they were therefore very much concerned with the possibility that another means might be found that would be morally acceptable.

The progesterone pill seemed to offer a solution to the problem. Theologians in general were impressed with the pill as a means whereby the biological action of the female menstrual cycle could be approximated and thus provide an opportunity to regulate birth through the resultant chemical action within the body which imitated "nature." It might be noted at this juncture that a theologian might recognize rhythm as the only licit method of contraception, yet allow the use of the progesterone pill for the purpose of regulating the menstrual cycle in order to make the practice of rhythm somewhat easier. Another, while holding to natural law as a norm and repudiating the use of a condom, might see the use of the pill as a way of capitalizing on man's inventive ability to create chemical compounds that duplicate the natural rhythm of the female menstrual cycle.

The author of this book, writing in *The Christian Century* on January 18, 1967, could find no value in this kind of distinction, for a chemical withholding of the ovum by the pill is not materially different from a mechanical withholding of the sperm by the condom. Nor, in this author's opinion, can an acceptable distinction be made between the rhythm method and either the pill or the condom, when it is maintained that the rhythm method harmonizes with natural law doctrine whereas the pill, the condom, and other methods of birth control do not.

The revisionists take a similar position in the matter of chemical withholding of the ovum and mechanical withholding of the sperm. They feel that neither method is any different from engaging in intercourse when, owing to the chemical operation of the woman's body, it is known that the meeting of sperm and ovum—necessary for conception —cannot take place.

Because the revisionist sees Pius XII's action as a thorough rejection of natural law doctrine, he feels that if one may exclude procreation by means of rhythm, then one may exclude it by means of other methods as well—provided that there is nothing intrinsically immoral in them—because what is at issue is not the method, but the intention involved in the decision to have intercourse while deliberately excluding the possibility of procreation. In view of this he insists that the acceptance of the rhythm method must inevitably lead to acceptance of other methods—again, provided that they are not intrinsically immoral.

In stressing intention as the critical factor in the matter of contraception, and declining to make distinctions among various methods employed, the revisionist is striking out in a new direction. He is maintaining that human ingenuity, the human rational mind, is being shut out from entrance into this area of ethical concern; and that supporters of the traditional line, who accept only rhythm as legitimate, are being unreasonable.

The traditionalist might reply that this is not a case of unreasonableness but one of faith taking man *beyond* reason, that this is an area of special sacrality which man is not permitted to submit to his own reason. He might say further that this area is so special because it deals with the preservation of the species, with the cooperation of man with God in the production of new human lives. On this account man's reason—although it can enter into and interfere in the sphere of the natural in many other areas— cannot do so here. There may or may not be rational justification for this, he might concede. But nevertheless the Church's tradition must be followed in preference to the reasoning of man.

In this connection it is interesting that the Second Vatican Council insisted that tradition does offer us a guideline, does have something fundamental to say. We may have to distinguish in the tradition what is valid from what is not; but there is a tradition, and it has some value. Even the most radical revisionist would be willing to acknowledge this. However, he might also argue that there is little or nothing that is unalterably absolute or immutable in the guidelines of that tradition; but rather that the tradition represents merely the conscientious efforts of Christians, basing their determinations on the extent of their knowledge, to articulate their commitment to the ethical in the concrete terms of specific situations. He might thus rightly contend that, while the history of the tradition is one of changes, its basic truth lies in Christ's own ethical message of love.

The Second Vatican Council did not intend to offer concrete solutions to the difficulties of married persons with respect to contraception because Pope Paul VI had decreed in the summer of 1964 that, pending the outcome of a study that was being made of the problems involved, he wished for no change in attitudes toward the regulations of Pius XII in this matter. Once before authority had intervened to halt theological speculation on this subject. In 1612 Claudius Aquaviva, superior general of the Society of Jesus, had ordered, under the precept of obedience and under penalty of excommunication and removal from any teaching office, that all Jesuits refrain from teaching or offering advice to the effect that there is any lightness of matter in sexual sins.[1]

Even though the Council did not speak directly to the issue of contraception, it certainly presented in its document on marriage in the modern world a series of guidelines which represented a radical departure from traditional modes of thought. The Council, influenced by the personalism of modern psychology, asserted that sexual intercourse is a personal act, a human act; that it concerns itself with love between persons, and embodies positive good and mutual enrichment. This was a markedly different view from that of many of the principal figures of the theological past.

Moreover, the Council, merely by responding to the need of parents to consider regulating the number of children they might have, was appropriating much of the thinking that had gone on in theological circles since 1951, and (as had Pius XII) was creating a "first" in theological history simply by speaking about the problem of birth control. For the Council asserted that each couple should determine the number of children they would have in light of their own good; the good of the children; the temporal and spiritual conditions of the time; their state of life; and the good of the communities of the family, society, and the Church. Even though the Council acknowledged an element of divine law in the Church's traditional teaching on contraception, it likewise acknowledged that laws on contraception could indeed be changed.

To some extent, therefore, what is at issue in this matter is—even in itself—a matter of authority. The question of whether or not this is the one area into which man's reason cannot enter is a legitimate one. Is or is not this area unique, sacred, because sexuality can be linked to the transmission of life itself? The answer is dependent upon authority. For precisely that reason the issue of contraception has developed into a conflict over the question of authority in the Church. As in any dispute of this nature, there are two things at stake: One is the prestige, the power, and the influence in the temporal sphere of those who head any institutionalized religion; the other, on the theological level, is the relationship between the authority of the believing community and the divine authority of its founder. The precise nature of that relationship is perennially debated among the founder's successors.

Thus the theological issue is, on the practical level, one concerning the relationship between the believer and the divine founder (with the exact role of the institution being a central question here). It is therefore an issue of faith. Is the individual related to God only through the Church? Can he be related to God directly and, if so, does the Church exist only to serve the individual and to minister to his needs? Can the Church act in any way as an impediment to direct relationship between the believer and God? These queries concerning authority are, in part at least, the subject matter of the next chapter. We shall also discuss the encyclical that prompted them—Pope Paul VI's *Humanae Vitae.*

## Footnotes 3

1. Letter of April 24, 1612, Archivum Romanum Societatis Jesu, Epp. NN 115, Fol. 498, cited by John T. Noonan, Jr., *Contraception: A History of its Treatment by the Catholic Theologians and Canonists* (Cambridge, Mass: Belknap Press of Harvard University Press, 1965), p. 358.

# 4
# REACTION
# AND REVOLT

One of the most difficult things that the modern mentality confronts is the antisex bias of the Roman Catholic ascetical mentality. It is a particular problem for the modern man because the new morality is the property of young people who have committed themselves to being genuinely human as contrasted with talking about and praising pseudo-virtues which no person really should either possess or wish to possess. The inexperience of youth is precisely the difficulty. And this difficulty is compounded by adults who try to shield the young from the very realities of which they must have at least a vicarious experience if they are to develop into whole individuals.

Part of the greatness of life is the struggle which goes on in man between his spiritual thirst for the infinite and his acute consciousness of his finiteness. The search to relieve the frustration created by that conflict is part of the religious quest of all men. And all great religions have turned at one time or another to asceticism and mortification of the flesh as a source of consolation, as an attempt to reach God, or out of a desire to rebel against the frustrations of being flesh.

Thus the antisex bias of Christianity can be fully understood only in the context of man's quest for salvation from the meaninglessness and unintelligibility of a world that dooms him to finitude and extinction. This is what makes it difficult for the inexperienced to fully understand the relevance of attitudes toward sexuality in religion. And this is likewise one reason why, in Christianity, sexuality has a tie to faith. To begin a rethinking of sexual ethics might indeed be the beginning of a rethinking of matters bearing upon the faith commitments of certain Christians. In the context of the historical progression of theological attitudes toward contraception, the papal encyclical *Humanae Vitae* therefore assumed a certain importance, for it tended—particularly as a consequence of the reaction it aroused—to draw attention to the close connection between Roman Catholic sexual morality and authority in the Church, and hence between attitudes toward sexuality and toward God on the level of faith itself.

The encyclical was greeted by some with unbelief, because it seemed to them that the pope was bent on dividing the very institution over which he presides. Others greeted it with despair, because they had had high hopes for a revision of the direction indicated by earlier statements. It was welcomed by those who saw in it signs of a return to "orthodoxy." But no one greeted it with more passion than those theologians who regarded it as theologically absurd.

Those seeking revision of the rule on contraception had been hoping that their ideas would be accepted. They had found widespread acceptance among both clergy and laity, but they specifically wanted papal acceptance. The papal response, when it finally came, was a refusal to innovate, despite the fact that those who wanted revision had implored the pope to heed their suggestions. Though sensitive to the Church's teaching authority, they were disappointed. Yet, that they sought papal acceptance and approval at all, and were so sensitive to the Church's teaching magisterium, is interesting. For the dynamic of protest, which repudiates institutional absolutizations in the name of an ever deeper understanding of the truth, cannot be judged by authority but only by the objective, rigorous criteria such as would be acceptable for judging the work of the professional theologian. This, however, was but another manifestation of a schizoid pattern in an effort at adjustment; the revisionists were saying in effect that they were not opposed to papal authority but only to its misuse.

The worldwide theological dissent that followed in the wake of the encyclical pointed to the growing cleavage within Roman Catholicism which the papal action had intensified. It became clear that the world's six hundred million Roman Catholics were at a turning point. No longer really united except by reason of their historical tradition, they now form two distinct camps regarding the issue of what it means to be a member in good standing of the institutional Church. The reason that the issue is so vital for Catholics is that a question that seemed at the beginning to be mainly one of sexual ethics was pushed by dissent from a papal encyclical into a question of authority. And in Roman Catholicism tradition has regarded authority as central to the ultimate religious question of faith itself.

Roman Catholic division and disenchantment has a broader context, however. It is a manifestation within Catholicism of a universal radicalization process that has been cutting across man's social, political, and religious life. The radicalization process referred to here is merely a part of man's total growth process whereby he comes to a greater, even more integrated self-consciousness and awareness. It has pitted man in his newer identity against man in his older identity. In his older identity man discovered who he was in relation to the forms, structures, and institutions of the society in which he found himself. In his newer identity man creates himself and his identity by creating his own relationships. He thus refuses to allow relationships to be predetermined for him; instead he calls into question the very forms and structures and institutions in relation to which others have found their identity and makes these accountable to himself.

Contemporary man is truly a creature of his own era, then, only if his life-style is radicalized—that is, only if he is existentially participating in the polarization taking place between the Establishment and those protesting against the established formal structure of human institutions. For contemporary man has a whole new psychic world view. He sees things differently than his forbears saw them. His new protests about things that his forbears accepted so readily—war, for example—illustrate this. Some of the objects of modern protest are not really more dreadful than some events of the past. But modern man *sees* them differently than his forbears saw or even *could* have seen them. For modernization, the process of radicalization and democratization, has created a totally *new* awareness. Modern man is a radically *changed* man. He is not merely better educated, although better education has contributed to his modernization; instead, to repeat, he possesses a radically altered psychic world view.

Modern man could thus feel profound disillusionment that the Church has persisted in reiterating the same platitudes, instead of deepening the ideals of marriage and expanding its goals and purview. In his *Humanae Vitae* Pope Paul VI maintains that in the task of transmitting life, husband and wife are not free to proceed completely at will, as though they could determine on their own the honest path to follow. Instead, he states, husband and wife must conform their activity to the intention of God which he sees as expressed in the very nature of marriage and "its acts." As idealistic as this may sound at first reading, it seems upon further reflection to be totally out of harmony with the reality of marriage—especially as it is widely and unexaminedly lived today. Is Paul really speaking to anyone in his encyclical? How many couples examine their marriages in this way?

In the same encyclical Paul goes further and insists that the natural law doctrine is founded upon an inseparable connection which he says is willed by God and unable to be broken by man: that between the two meanings of the conjugal act—the unitive and the procreative, as he calls them. At least Paul appreciates the problem; but the whole thrust of revisionist thinking is that man can broaden the scope of his enjoyment of sexual union by insuring that that union will be *non*procreative.

Is Paul's essentialist approach really relevant theological thinking for the modern problem of responsible parenthood? Is there not a genuine conflict between the various conditions of modern life which require birth regulation and the legitimate use of sexually expressed human love for its other licit purposes?

Since World War II and the experience with nazism, it is commonplace to see supposedly legitimately constituted authority questioned, protested against, and even openly defied through public civil disobedience. Moral protests are continually being leveled against discrimination, war, the draft. The conflict in the Church is thus part of the total universal process occurring at this time.

The radicalization process in Catholicism is vital because there is a widespread desire on the part of the community that the function of religion be relevant. The search for relevance has resulted in the destruction of irrelevant forms. The question is how far will such destruction go. How much can be called into question without destroying the religion itself? The distinction between those who will go to extremes in questioning beliefs and those who have already stopped questioning serves to draw the line between the protesters and the Establishment who are currently in conflict, not only over plans and programs but over form, structure, and being itself.

The danger in calling into question the very forms in which men have traditionally discovered their identity is that one's life might itself sink into formlessness and loss of self-identification. While there is an ultimate limit to the Christian's commitment—namely, faith—and while he may call into question not only the external trappings of institutionalized religion but also belief-statements, he may not fell beliefs arbitrarily. There is, however, an evolution of doctrine which can and must go forward. And that evolution will often require that beliefs (not faith) be called into question. What has been unfortunate and mistaken is the view that it is the proper role of the magisterium of the Church to resolve philosophical arguments about the way in which the community tries to articulate its faith in Christ through statements of belief. These attempts of the community, in its teaching role with respect to the formation of its members, to articulate its faith in Christ are credal statements subject to revision and evolution. The mistake has been to attribute to such beliefs the ultimacy of faith and, in the final analysis, to attribute to the legitimate teaching authority upon which the beliefs were formulated a similar ultimacy. This was the source of the hierarchical heresy of institutionalism.

And so man is witnessing the end of an era, a time when political, social, and religious ideas are being polarized largely as the consequence of a worldwide movement toward the radicalization of human life. Like any period of revolution, it is a time fraught with an anxiety that reaches to the very core of man's being, an anxiety that is the source of man's religious quest to resolve the problems of death, meaninglessness, and sin.

With respect to the encyclical *Humane Vitae,* the conflict among Catholics is not merely a difference of opinion on a minor issue of sex ethics. It strikes at the very heart of what many have understood as their faith commitment. For some, that was an understanding that put the ecclesiastical institution above the revolutionary Christ, and institutional teaching above the teaching of Jesus.

Division over the encyclical, therefore, exists on many levels. It cuts across the older estimates of authority, freedom, sexuality, and, ultimately, faith itself. The liberals are challenging traditional notions about sexuality and in doing so are striking a nerve, for sexuality is a sensitive issue. In light of the recent encyclical, however, the liberals are likewise challenging ecclesiastical authority as it is viewed by many of those in power in the institution. The liberals see their challenge as the appropriate work of scholars seeking a fuller understanding of the truth; but the power structure sees it as an undermining of the very foundations of religion. The reason is that older generations took their institutional forms most seriously, and their institution-oriented understanding of faith itself is presently in danger of being totally shattered. The identity of some has been disintegrated. In the search merely to integrate themselves as persons, many have in effect walked away from religious observance; others —such as priests and religious—often more sensitive and more deeply committed, have felt compelled to reject their past *in toto*.

Some religious have become completely disillusioned with the institutional Church. They feel that the dogmatism with which one man's ethical opinion was taught has led them astray. They had molded and directed their lives on account of their "belief" in an ethic that is now being seen as relative, human, outdated. They cannot turn back the clock and refashion their lives. Bitter and angry, many of them now hate the Church. They had studied pious authors diligently; they had absorbed their spiritual reading with care. They had meditated and prayed, and accepted the silence of God and the babel of churchmen speaking in God's name.

Now they realize why God was silent: he had spoken enough by his word of creation. He had made man in his own image, and endowed him with the infinite potentialities of reason and free will. It was not God at all, but only other men who had made slaves of their fellowmen. And the pattern was repeated through the ages and in nonreligious areas as well. The guilt-peddlers would not soon be out of business. So long as there could be an immature faith there could be a child of whom advantage might be taken. Those who wished to serve God might be forced into the service of an anti-God.

Still others are desperately trying to shield themselves from such pain by hiding from the light. They seek refuge from the effects of radicalization through entrenchment behind the protective walls of an ever more adamant assertion of the old order in which the ultimacy of the institution guaranteed the comfort of certainty in theological matters.

Any attempt to resolve the conflict and to restore the balance requires a careful reassessment of the Christian's commitment to faith in Jesus; for, as previously mentioned, the issue of contraception has expanded beyond the confines of sexual ethics to become the focal point for significant conflict within Catholicism. Any issue might have served to test the extent of authoritarianism within the Church. Yet quarrels over liturgical reforms, however violent, never precipitated the broad challenge to authority that is being raised over contraception.

One reason for contraception's apparent suitability to its role as catalyst in the contention between the dissenters and Church authorities is the clear fact of its relevance. Contraception has such a widespread, personal importance that it received the interested support of enough Catholics to make their dissent far more significant than the dissent of a small group, even of articulate theologians.

Whether or not the radicalization process within the Church will be pushed further in connection with the issue of contraception will undoubtedly depend upon the extent to which the majority does or does not remain dissatisfied. If, despite the encyclical, some face-saving method of backing down from the pope's stand can be found, then this issue may not be carried to a final resolution. It will, however, have served as an important step in the process by which the community grows to self-consciousness in Christ.

Actually, there is an ideological fight going on in the Church, although many are reluctant to admit this. From the Establishment's point of view, it has the overtones of a fight for power, wealth, and social control. The reason is that control of sexual mores, family mores, and the attitudes that center around the use of sexuality, can be extremely significant for the control of attitudes in general, for the preservation of society as presently structured, and for the maintenance of an economic system in which wealth is more easily accumulated and held back from those who bear the burden of producing and rearing offspring within certain social confines. But the fight is highly theological as well. It revolves around the question of the death of other kinds of absolutes apart from the natural law doctrine. Philosophically speaking, it is a struggle for a new world view.

But if this question of sexual ethics and the conflict it has caused are indeed capable of pushing the radicalization process within Roman Catholicism to its limits, what makes this possible? The theoretical model at stake here depends upon the repudiation of the "natural law" doctrine, which is now generally ignored as irrelevant in the context of a modern era, which is technological rather than natural. Concern with the "natural" in sexual relationships was a concern with the external, with outward form in interpersonal relationships; with the appearances, the trappings, the accidentals of human relationships rather than with their depth, their reality, and their substance. It was a concern that was biological, and it occupied the society's interest on account of what were felt to be distasteful consequences of a socially disruptive nature.

Modern psychological theory is far more concerned with what one does with his interpersonal relationships than it is with the mere form that the relationship can assume. Modern theological thought is far more concerned with the way in which relationships are used—that is, for good or for evil.

Consequently there is now less interest in whether or not two people deeply in love are validly married, refrain from "artificial" contraception, or are of different sexes, than there is in whether or not they are productively using their relationship in a loving, truly Christian way.

Translation of this model to the broader area of the Roman Catholic community at large in its specifically religious context yields an interesting result. Since the context is one of faith, what must be at issue—if there is indeed sufficient similarity between contexts to validate the model theory—is a question of form versus substance. And this is indeed at issue. What began in the liturgical reform movement as an attempt to alter forms in order to reflect a more worthwhile reality has ended in the repudiation of the institution on the basis of its concern for form and form alone. Those who might reject the institutional Church are doing so on the grounds that its very form-oriented structure is a hindrance to genuine Christian substance.

The reason that the rethinking of sexual ethics has an importance beyond the purely ethical question involved is that it raises questions about the Roman Catholic's accustomed understanding of his relationship to the Church. It goes directly against the concept of a fixed, dogmatic viewpoint. It is anti-institutional because it is antidogmatic, because it opposes any position not subject to change and not flexible enough to be subject to reason. Some will call it heresy because it goes against the very concept of "ecclesiastical faith."

Institutions can seem "perfect." They persist; they lose the "imperfect" character of individual humans. The institution survives even its prophets. And thus it attains a kind of absolutism which has about it many of the characteristics which men ordinarily attribute to their deities: immutability, perfect truth, eternality, omnipotence. To go against this absolute quality, even in that which is clearly man-made and even in the pursuit of Christ himself, can therefore be called "heresy." For it represents an attack upon that God which, in the minds of some, the merely human institution has become. Consequently whatever goes against the view of the institution as that which can do no wrong, as that which has captured the divine, is anti-Church, that is, anti-institutionalized Church.

Disciplinary matters like liturgical forms, clerical celibacy, fasts, and abstinences can easily be dropped from observance. And though beliefs—that is, credal statements—in which the community attempts to articulate its faith in order to assist in the religious formation of the believer, ought not to be dropped without reason, such doctrines, as pointed out previously, are subject to evolution as the community progresses to greater integration in awareness, self-consciousness, and relationship to God. Thus the believing community of Christians follows the same patterns of evolutionary development as do individuals and the entire race.

The evolution of doctrine means that beliefs can be better understood, and this may mean the death of false inferences. As a fuller understanding is attained, however, the community is still engaged in the effort to express in words the essence of its faith commitment. This effort will never achieve perfection, but a continuous striving toward that goal must be made. For if each individual is to relive for himself the New Testament experience of finding God in Jesus, he must be made receptive to Jesus' message through the formation which the community offers him.

The Church does, therefore, have a legitimate teaching mission because it has the obligation to show forth to humanity a community of Christian concern in which all men can see an accurate and enlightening reflection of life lived according to the Christian model. Even if all credal statements fell into disuse, however unlikely that may be, faith would still remain. For just as no linguistic or philosophical formulation can ever adequately capture the meaning of faith, neither can any finite human statement ever refute the infinite possibilities which faith opens up to man.

The radicalization process is thus directed against giving to the institutional structure of the Church an absolutist authority that in effect supersedes the authority of Christ himself. And it is this which has constituted the institutional heresy of Roman Catholicism.

In the case of Penance, for example, there has been a turning away from frequent observance because of dissatisfaction with the traditional understanding of that sacrament as a kind of magical ritual for the cleansing of the soul. If it is to have any real relevance to the fundamental structure of the Christian's religious commitment through faith in Christ, Penance must be seen as a credal restatement on the part of the community of its trust in Christ's good news of salvation. It is thus an acknowledgment to the penitent on the part of Christ's mystical body, and hence on behalf of Christ himself, that the penitent, though sinner, is yet justified and saved by the merits of Jesus.

If such an interpretation is valid, then the suggestion that the usual confessional form be replaced by general absolution of an entire group of persons is a step away from the common impression that the penitent must personally detail his sins to a priest in order to receive forgiveness. The negative effect of this impression was that it caused Catholics to feel that a specific institutional system of ritual was the channel of salvation rather than that any suitable form which brought together two or more members in the name of Jesus was a guarantee of Jesus' saving presence in our midst. In other words, every insistence upon a ritualistic form places emphasis on the accidental, magical aspects of the mystery of salvation by faith instead of upon those elements whereby the individual signifies by his actions the desire to give himself totally to Jesus in faith and submission as sinner.

If the issue of contraception has been a *cause célèbre* because of its relevance to human life, there are also other areas in which the Church could beneficially affect people's lives but has not done so. In every case in which the Church —often because it is hemmed in by legalisms, by restrictions, and by forms—fails to recognize that her members are human persons with human problems, it is antihuman. And to the extent to which the Church is antihuman, she is likewise anti-Jesus and anti-God. This anti-Christ element in the Church itself comes into existence whenever structures and forms take precedence over human relations and over the love which Christ insists must typify his members in their relations to one another and to God.

To conceive of the priesthood, for example, as the duly consecrated collection of the ritually ordained, and hence valid, legally established representatives of God, might have the dangerous effect of putting God at a distance rather than bringing him to us. If the priest is truly "another Christ," it is not because he is an emissary touched from on high, but because he is a representative of the human persons who comprise the believing community. The priest represents this community, the mystical body of Christ, rather than the Church understood as merely a human institution. To be confronted in any sacramental form by the priest is to be confronted by the community. To confront the priest is to confront one's fellowmen. And by reason of Christ's promise, where two or more are gathered together in his name, Christ is present, not through priestly magic but through human meeting. What is important, then, is that the community's chosen sacramental forms are effective for bringing its members closer to Christ.

This is not to deny that there is room for an institutional Church. But such a Church must exist to help men function better together as humans, not to impede that functioning. The institutional Church has lost her proper direction if she attempts to set herself above her members, to separate herself from her own humanness, and to interfere with the relational confrontation of human to human whereby man contacts God himself.

Those who complain of priests not differentiating themselves by means of a distinct garb, for example, have missed the point. Priests who don ordinary clothes are trying to be more approachable so that we can more easily realize that they, as representatives of the community, are fulfilling the human function into which the divine enters when two or more assemble in Christ's name.

At the present time there is a decided movement away from the institutional Church. Part of the reason for this trend is clearly the fact that large numbers of contemporary Roman Catholics no longer find the forms and formulations of the institutional Church and its hierarchy meaningful or relevant for them in the circumstances of their daily lives. Too often representatives of the institutional Church have functioned in a vacuum. They have moved and spoken within a universe of thought and discourse populated essentially by philosophical verities and essences rather than by existential facts of life and the realties of human situations.

Consequently, pronouncements that emanate from the magisterium, that is, from the pope or from national conferences of bishops, are received by the people with utter indifference. Thus the two groups—the hierarchy on the one hand and the laity on the other—are not communicating. The hierarchical statements might be repeated or new ones might be made from now until the end of time. But the laity is not hearing what the hierarchy is saying. Perhaps the reason is that the hierarchy has failed to listen to what the laity has been saying.

Without attempting an exhaustive analysis of why there is no communication between the hierarchy and the laity, it should nevertheless be realized that the two groups obviously stand in no relation to one another. There is an ever-increasing unwillingness, on the part of American Catholics at least, to be dominated by a Roman pontiff who seems forever destined to be an Italian. It is difficult for Americans to believe that the Holy Spirit repeatedly chooses Italians for the papacy over all the possible candidates of other nationalities.

In the case of the conferences of bishops, too, there is a breakdown in communications. The bishops are not speaking to the laity because, ironically, the way in which they are related to the institutionalized Church structure makes it impossible for them to relate to the very people they are supposed to serve. This inability of bishops and priests to relate to the people stems from a life-style for which they have been groomed from the first day of their seminary training. That training tended far more to take them out of and away from the world, and to separate them from so-called worldly values, than it did to prepare them for serving *in* the world as the leaven for transforming worldly values into spiritual ones. The result has been to create a new set of *clerical* values.

An important part of seminary training concerns priestly celibacy. It is highly significant that celibacy is the specific ascetical practice imposed upon every man desirous of becoming a priest, for it tends to set priests apart from other men, not as the uniform of the Roman collar does, but by making them seem preterhuman and therefore superior to laymen.

Although the sacrifice of the explicitly venereal use of sexuality can indeed be a worthwhile one, it is not only unrealistic, but actually dangerous, to make it a prerequisite for priestly ordination. The insistence upon this prerequisite has led to disorders among priests as well as to an unfortunate understanding of celibacy. The issue is not the connection between sexuality and passion, but the connection between sexuality and humanity. And any step in the direction of desexualization is automatically dehumanizing when it is a demand upon *all* candidates for the priesthood rather than the carefully thought out ascetical sacrifice of a particular individual.

Every step away from the priest's humanity is a step away from the humanity of those whom he is pledged to serve in the name of Jesus. Every such step leads toward division rather than toward unity. Has this not been the reason why some priests are so uncompassionate in the face of the laity's human needs? So able to totally divorce themselves from the existential concerns of people and to think in terms of essentialist, rationalist absolutes, unmoved by human consideration? And is this not also the source of the complaint on the part of the laity that the institutional Church has indeed lost its relevance? If the priests themselves are separated from their people, even if this separation is the result of their having been placed on a pedestal, then how can we expect the people to draw close to God through the institutional Church? Must we not expect instead that the institutional Church will begin to look like an obstacle to real union with Christ?

Because of the link between the Roman Catholic's view of sexuality and his general world view, the controversy over birth control and the dissent from the encyclical *Humanae Vitae* have become the battering-rams in the push against the institutional authoritarian structure. To repeat, there is grave danger inherent in an emphasis on celibacy which holds out as a *better* way, not a carefully chosen ascetical practice, but an antihuman and anti-Christian attempt to make men angels instead of saints.

Roman Catholicism's antisex bias is the source of the attitude that those who enjoy the use of their sexual faculties are somehow inferior to those who do not. Yet to use one's sexuality is merely to be human just as to use one's arms to lift is merely to perform a human act. Those who isolate themselves from their sexuality isolate themselves from the existential reality of being human. Thus, by reason of an ability to close their eyes and minds to existential realities, they seem able also to make declarations that clearly represent ivory-tower rationalizations devoid of realistic pertinence. One of the realities they obviously overlook is the fact that renunciation of sexual pleasures can be over-evaluated to a point where it creates serious disorders.

## Humanae Vitae and Its Implications

When Pope Paul VI issued his encyclical after a long period of hesitation, he tied his statement on contraception to the married couple's duty to transmit human life.

In part, at least, the pope is obviously committed to the preservation of a value system in which much of life's meaning centers upon a biologically dictated concern with the continuation of the human species. Thus much of the individual's attainment of meaning, purpose, and fulfillment in life comes directly out of his role as transmitter of life. He takes purpose and meaning from his struggle to get his offspring started on their own production of offspring. The parent wishes to see them "off to a good start" and "settled down" with the right partner. The quality of life that each parent ultimately wants for his offspring has, however, become the foremost problem in modern urban society, and responsibility to children already born has created the desire to have no more or, at least, "no more right now."

It is crucial to realize that it is this kind of value-system that is at issue, despite the many contradictions within it. Life is the supreme value of earthly existence. Few would quarrel with that. Yet the afterlife is a greater value, though a noncontradicting one. For the propagation of human bodies means the propagation of human souls. And the implication has traditionally been that the quality of this life can be sacrificed to the propagation of candidates for heaven (though little mention is made of the fact that such souls are similarly candidates for hell as well). Yet—and this detracts somewhat from the absoluteness of the value at issue here—the "spiritual perfection" of an individual takes precedence over his life-producing possibilities. It is not sinful, but virtuous, that some persons voluntarily embrace continence rather than produce human souls, even though they are able to do so. The religious value which gave meaning to what would otherwise be a meaningless cycle of species-propagation bows to another religious value—that is, the choice of personal continence. The cycle of propagating offspring who will then propagate others who will in turn propagate others, and so on, is what gives life its meaning. Even those who do not propagate are given meaningful refuge, since they can see their own purpose as tied to the service of this process.

In brief, then, the purpose of life is to keep life going—

not "this life" in any strictly personal sense, but the life of the species. But the purpose of the propagation of the species is unclear. That difficulty, however, and the correlative difficulty of a lack of personal fulfillment in "this life," are resolved by resorting to "afterlife" concepts of immortality. There is a biblical command of sorts: "Increase and multiply." But, obviously, not all are bound to it. Life under any circumstances is tolerable, it is said, because there is an afterlife. But that afterlife might well be hell. Moreover, God does not seem to have said that he wants any particular number.

The pope's statement was therefore unfortunate because it contradicted well-reasoned theological thought on the subject. In addition it killed the hope that—under the impetus toward openness in theological speculation which was thought to be encouraged by Vatican II—the Church might present a relevant, practical set of moral guidelines rather than a mere reiteration of the old view that had not only been challenged, but overturned, by the theological tour de force of the past decade and the widespread acceptance of the revisionist position by both priests and laymen.

The statement was also criticized because it went against the majority view of the pope's own commission on birth control, and because it seemed insensitive to the population explosion. Clearly it served to highlight the dependence of the sexual ethic upon authority, a very sensitive subject among Catholics.

With respect to the encyclical, the pope was *not* making in it an infallible pronouncement—that is, he was not speaking explicitly ex cathedra—but responding to requests that he give his own opinion on an issue that had caused much controversy. The response, as noted, represents nothing new. It is neither a change in the direction of revision, nor a change which makes earlier statements into matters of faith.

The pope assured the world that his opinion was the outcome of considerable thought and much agonizing concern. Quite naturally, those who wished for an infallible pronouncement try to make the encyclical's statements as dogmatic-sounding as possible. But no matter what is said, if the statement is not infallible—and it is not—then Catholics are not obliged to hold the view as a credal statement if there are good reasons for holding a different view. And there are such reasons. Moreover, those who say that the statement "approaches" infallibility or is "nearly" infallible are dealing in semantic nonsense. A statement is infallible or it is not.

The encyclical is the pope's admission that he cannot see his way through to a revision of the ethical guidelines of his predecessors. As a statement coming from a pope (who might reasonably be considered, ex officio, as the "first theologian" of the Church) it is, of course, worthy of consideration. Apparently by his own wish, however, it is not the final word. It is not definitive. But then the questions arise: Since the encyclical says nothing that is new, why was it written at all? Why did the pope not make an infallible pronouncement? Was it that he feared a genuine schism if he had done so?

Moreover, if the encyclical were not an attempt to assert papal authority, would there not have been several alternatives to that of making a pronouncement that would please neither side very much? However weak, and even if ultimately doomed to reversal by future developments, the encyclical is an attempt to assert authority. In a period of worldwide revolution it is a reactionary attempt to hold on to the old order.

For the individual the practical effect of this attempt will depend not so much upon the doctrine as upon his own view of his Church and its authority. Those with a conservative viewpoint in this connection will see the statement as so "close to infallible" as to be normative for them; they may disobey, to be sure, but their conscience will hurt when they do. Those who regard the statement as definitely not infallible, as not normative for them in the light of opposing views, will consider the issues as remaining in dispute and will follow their conscience in the matter.

This is not to say that, even for the latter group, the tradition of looking to the pope for theological leadership of the believing community is dead. But persons looking to leaders wish to be led forward. They look for new ground to be broken, for relevant solutions to pressing issues when old views have proved grossly inadequate. By definition, contemporary man is striving for self-awareness by calling into question every aspect of the old order.

The older authoritarian, paternalistic view of the Church may have been satisfactory even shortly before Vatican II. But the spirit which John XXIII infused into the Church by his calling of the Council has made older views intolerable to a new generation. Today's Catholics are hearing and responding to new theological voices, often the voices of theologically trained laymen. In times past within Roman Catholicism the theologians, virtually always priests, have themselves been part of the rigid hierarchical structure of the institutional Church. They have therefore not enjoyed the freedom to speak out at will in an expression of their beliefs. Some have been "silenced" by their ecclesiastical superiors. A medieval notion of authority made this possible, but that notion is not shared today by most well-educated Catholics.

The effect is a new age neither of faith as opposed to reason nor of reason as opposed to faith. It is rather an age in which there is a new emphasis on both. Faith has become heightened but radicalized as the believer's response to the absurd meaninglessness of a world without God and to the message of Jesus. Reason has been given full sway as the tool that God has given men in order that they might decide in freedom what they must do to live up to their destiny as creatures made in his image.

In such an age a blind "faith" in an institution governed by mortal men cannot long survive, and another attempt to assert authority could mark the beginning of a new division within Christianity. We have witnessed efforts on the part of certain ecclesiastics to assert their authority at the terrible price of division, disenchantment, destruction. This is tragic in a time of ecumenism and *aggiornamento.* For there is really a new estimation today of what theology is. The older generation saw theology as essentially static. They rejoiced in the doctrine of "papal infallibility" as a kind of guarantee, not that the spirit would abide always with the community as Christ had promised, but almost as a kind of magical assurance that the institutional Church would possess an infallible, divinely-bestowed pipeline to truth. Their concept hinged upon the institution's having somehow captured the divine within its walls, which is precisely what Luther had protested against. They saw theology as a set of philosophically elaborated truths written in manuals rather than as a search for truth under the light of a man's existential commitment to faith in Christ.

And this is why there is a quality of faith at issue here. Christian faith is not a fixed, firm, almost rationally demonstrable consent of the will to the propaganda of an institution. It is a tenuous, existential leap in which a person, despite his own agnosticism and doubts, believes Jesus Christ.

It is admittedly quite comfortable and satisfying to put one's trust in an institution, but Christ asks for trust in him. And it is a trust not in the power of the sacraments because they are almost magical in their efficacy but, instead, a trust in the power of the sacraments because Jesus has promised to be present in whatever it is that two or three gathered together in his name do by way of action symbolizing and, in fact, acting out truly their faith in him.

The faith of some Christians is not in Jesus but in the Church or in theology. Yet even if religion is right, theology may be wrong. Theology must be distinguished from religious commitment; it is, after all, *only* theology. Those anxious to initiate heresy trials have traditionally put too much faith in the man-made aspects of religious beliefs. They want more certitude about their salvation than faith by its very nature can deliver. Faith is a mystery because it is the relation between God and man, and the mystery in human life is the mystery of what God is. Saint Paul says we are saved by faith. If this is so, it is faith in Jesus, not faith in theology. Those who fail to realize that—even if all the speculations of theologians are totally wrong—faith is enough, are not searching for the truth. What they are doing is defending their truth which makes their Christ a God who can be put at the service of men capable of being manipulated, threatened, and cajoled.

Controversy has surrounded the theological debate over birth control because the change of ethics proposed by the advocates of revision actually amounts to saying that what had been almost universally deemed seriously sinful by theologians is presently being seen as quite virtuous.

Apart from the theological controversy, however, the present conflict is as serious as it is principally because it represents a head-on collision between two aspects of religious belief. And where belief is even subconsciously the real issue, whether in politics or religion, tensions can run very high indeed. For belief is always concerned with the individual's solution of the most important of all questions—namely, the religious one: Is there any ultimate meaning to my life beyond the purview of my earthly sojourn, or am I in fact merely an insignificant drop in the ocean of beings in a universe already millions of years old? Perhaps the following will help to explain these two kinds of conflicting beliefs. One is belief in Jesus, in his promise of salvation, and in his guarantee that he would abide with his Church, and send the Spirit to protect and guide the community of those who believe in him. The other belief is belief in Jesus, in his promise of salvation, and in his guarantee that he would be found with the institutional Church, and would send the Spirit to protect and guide those ministers responsible for the welfare of that Church.

The disagreement has been well characterized as a conflict over authority. In fact the polarization of views is brought into focus by the theological problem of interpreting the 1870 Vatican I doctrine of the "infallibility of the pope." Some see this doctrine as a guarantee of a divinely certified, absolute inability to err on the part of the pope whenever he speaks explicitly ex cathedra to the Roman Catholic world on any matter of faith or morals. Others see it as the acknowledgment on the part of the believing community of their faith in Jesus' promise to send the Spirit to guide and protect them lest they ultimately fail. In the one case the doctrine is seen as declaring the infallibility of one man's pronouncements about essences; in the other it is seen as declaring the indefectibility of the believing community's existential commitment to its Lord Jesus. What heightens the conflict even more is the fact that we are emerging from an era in which the former view was unchallenged.

It is critical to realize that Christ promised to send the Spirit to the Church. This promise is recorded in Scripture and is of importance in our tradition. It is the promise of Christ Himself that the Church, the believing community which he founded, will not fail.

This is what infallibility really means. It does not mean hierarchical dominance. This is where the difficulty has been. And this is why a conflict over authority is possible in the Church today. In the past this difficulty has led to an invalid concept of faith, to the great "heresy of institutionalism" in Roman Catholicism.

If the radicalization process moves us back beyond credal statements to faith itself, at least in the sense that we see beliefs as subject to change, then clearly faith is the ultimate ground we reach. Yet, while such faith frees us from perverted pseudo-faith in institutional pronouncements as the ground of our existential commitment to God (on account of a heretical divinization of the institution), it prompts us to formulate our own credal statements about Jesus and the nature of our commitment to him.

If the Spirit is to be given to the whole Church, conceived of as the believing community, then it is the duty of all believers to stand up and be heard on all important issues. It is their moral responsibility to Christ and to the Church to exert their power to insure that right triumphs. Ordinary believers are not theologians; they are not Church administrators. They are the Church, and the theologians and administrators are their servants. But the great "institutional heresy" of Roman Catholicism has been to make the servants into the masters. It is a heresy because it is founded upon a mistaken principle which gave to the hierarchy a sort of absolutist corner on theological truth. It took its final form in the doctrine of infallibility, as traditionally interpreted, a concept which represents something vastly different from what the believing community may really have been trying to say —namely, that the community continues to believe in Christ's promise to abide with the Church and to send the Spirit to guide and protect it from ultimate failure.

In the present circumstances, on the basis of the above analysis, some Catholics will not walk away from the Church as so many have done in this difficult time; they will instead take a firm stand within the Church and let their views be known, in order that the Spirit may be free to speak through them. It is always difficult to register a protest against that which one loves. It is so much easier to sever a relationship than to offer criticism that is intended to be constructive, but which one fears may destroy the relationship. Yet some Catholics feel that the time has come to make it clear that one cannot in conscience lend his support to any institution that he believes is dangerously in error.

The call of Jesus is a call to service and love—service of God and love of neighbor. It is a call to greatness, a call to being truly human. It is also a call to sacrifice. Man is made to love, to commit his entire being. Some Catholics feel guided by the Spirit to commit the love inside of them to the task of standing up for what they know is right. Others, though, have given up hope entirely as far as the institutional Church is concerned. They first thought that the plea for relevance might be heard and answered with reforms that would lead to reconciliation between the Establishment and those who dissented from institutionalism in the name of Jesus. Now, however, this group feels that the institution is by its very nature anti-Christ, and that no reconciliation is therefore possible. They have concluded that the sprawling Roman Catholic giant is dead, at least spiritually.

Responsive to the image of God within him, the believer aspires to the positive actualization of man's infinite potential for good. Tired of being told that he is evil and must repent, modern man insists that to imitate Christ he must seek the good and do it. He is convinced that there is no such thing as a "natural" mode of being to which and by which he is shackled, but that it is only the substance of what one does with one's being which is redemptive; so he has thrown off the very chains which bound him to the modes and forms of the institution. Aware that his being is constituted by his relationships and that to the extent that he consciously directs the choice of these relationships he creates himself anew, modern man is acutely conscious of the fact that an all-absorbing concern with the degree to which his relationships conform to a given "natural" form or mode is a superficial, hypocritical, and egotistical means of seeking security. He rejects this absorption with the form of the relationships that are the constituent elements of his being and concerns himself with the way in which he uses these relationships for the love of God seen in his neighbor.

It might be pointed out that rejection of corrupt institutionalism follows the same model as that of the revisionists' rejection of natural law doctrine as the basis for a sexual ethic. To contend that revisionist acceptance of contraception as ethical is the basis for the radicalization permeating Roman Catholicism requires a model which fits both of these processes. Finding the model is not difficult, however, and what is clear is that this model really represents something of a protestantization of Roman Catholicism. This does not mean that the Roman Catholic Church is turning into a kind of Protestant one. This is not at issue. Protestant churches are just as institutionalized as the Roman Catholic. However, what Martin Luther started in the sixteenth century is really being completed or perfected today by the process of radicalization or polarization that is going on. To that extent this process can be called a protestantization or, to put it another way, this is the Protestant dynamic in operation. It operates for the revisionist theologians who accept contraception as ethical insofar as their revision represents a substitution of reason for biology; but these same theologians simultaneously recognize that even if the revision is accepted, the doctrine is always open to further revision. This is precisely the Protestant dynamic at work.

Luther's protest was against the idea that the institution could somehow capture and dispense the divine at will. What is happening in the modern radicalization process within Roman Catholicism is that individuals are standing up in the name of Jesus, or in the name of the way in which they have rediscovered Jesus, just as Luther did when he thought he had rediscovered the word of God in Scripture. And they are, like Luther, protesting that the rediscovered true message of Jesus, a message of living out and acting out the search for goodness and love of one's neighbor, is lacking within the institutional structure. This is why, for example, a group of priests in an American diocese recently accused the diocese of following a racist line. What these priests were expressing, it would seem, is that the institutional structure is not oriented toward actually living out the revolutionary message of Christianity. The reason is that Christ's message, a message of poverty, makes no provision for the continuation of an institution in time based upon its economic position in the world.

There is a similarity, however, between the revisionist theologians' acceptance of contraception as ethical and the insistence by the priests mentioned in the foregoing paragraph upon Christian action in preference to form. The former reject the idea that there is some sort of natural form which sexual activities must follow, and the dissenters from the institutional are likewise saying that the institution follows form without substance. Just as the revisionists reject the natural law doctrine because of its concern with the forms of relationships instead of what one does with relationships, so too those who protest against the institutional establishment of the Church are rejecting an insistence upon form, especially institutional form, and insisting themselves upon acting out truly the Gospel message of Jesus which is a message of love of neighbor. And to love one's neighbor is to live one's faith in Jesus.

When the believer believes on account of his own weakness, his belief is a crutch. But when he believes despite his own strength, then his belief is the leap into the air of the lame man made whole. Faith as a crutch deforms man; it makes him less than whole. When faith is adult, it makes man truly human and thus truly godly; for man as such is created in God's own image.

It is a fact that, while dogmatic ethical pronouncements emanating from Church hierarchies might speak to many of those born before the end of the First World War, they carry little weight with any significant percentage of post-World War I generations. In particular, many of those born after the Great Depression feel that authoritarian pronouncements from a highhanded hierarchy will have no real effect practically or theoretically—unless it is to increase alienation from institutionalized religion.

Because man's great glory is that he alone among God's creatures has reason and hence can consciously direct his own destiny, he is freed from the burden of the unnatural. But he must shoulder the even greater burden of choosing, in accordance with the highest motive of conscience, that which is right. Thus Christ's message of faith, while it frees man from taboo, from magic, from anxiety, and from the evils of institutionalism, can never be separated from his ethical message. This makes clear that man's reason-grounded freedom releases him from the bondage of law so that he might be free to pursue more faithfully the goals of Christian conscience, to create himself in terms of his relationships to others after the model Christ sets out for him, and to be always toward others what he wants others to be toward him.

# 5
# A NEW
# DIRECTION

In the present situation, one has a choice. If one can abstract from the ideological fight in progress and escape embroilment in the theological controversy over orthodoxy and authority and institutionalism, then the choice is to heed the pope and the traditional interpretation of sexual ethics, or to opt for the revisionist tack on contraception and with it arrive at the destruction of the natural law doctrine and the recognition of the need to rethink the *whole* of sexual ethics.

Acceptance of a sense of option carries with it enough inherent power to amount to a rejection of the natural law doctrine simply because that doctrine is so absolute and so static as to be really a construct of an entirely different universe of discourse. Its survival is impossible in the new theological universe of discourse in which a more dynamic concept of establishing ethical values and rules holds sway, and where there is room for development, innovation, and evolution in ethics. Guidelines for choosing among the alternative solutions to any situation of ethical conflict are not fixed absolutes. It is left to each individual, on the basis of his own personal commitment to Christianity, to decide for himself how he must act in a given set of circumstances. He is not made to feel that he is bound to conform to behavior determined by Augustine, Thomas Aquinas, or Alphonsus Liguori. For accompanying the evolutionary development of man and his understanding—not only of his world and himself, but also of the depth of the Christian message—is a necessary evolution of circumstances; consequently circumstances, while they may seem similar, can never really be for modern man the same as they were for Christians of an earlier era. And this is true of things both material and psychic.

Because this evolution took place so slowly over a long span of time, most men may not have been aware of it. It is far easier to understand it in a period like our own, when change is so rapid that outmoded and outdated ideas are easily discernible. Within this new theological universe of discourse which offers room for ethical development and evolution, there is a new choice: a choice to rethink the ethics of sexuality within a framework of freedom in which no individual is confined to the narrowly defined area of what some see as the limits of orthodoxy.

The currently prevailing sense of option in sexual matters is based principally upon man's psychic achievement of a new world view within the context of which theologians have moved towards an acceptance of nonprocreative intercourse as ethical. This has been the work of the revisionists. And while there are those who cannot or will not accept their conclusions, those who do accept them have much work to do. The rethinking and the new conclusions do not necessarily mean a change of ideals. They signify only an end to the exploitation of guilt feelings as a means of enforcing ideals, a means resorted to when the consequences of the ordinary use of sex were *understood* to be always very grave indeed. It does not follow, however, that acts formerly prohibited on account of their intrinsic immorality are no longer prohibited simply because the older *understanding* about them has been discarded. It does, however, mean a drastic alteration of the character and hence the intention of any prohibition. In particular it means a clear-cut distinction between warnings against what *may* be tawdry, antisocial, or empty; and warnings against what *is* immoral, sinful, and in violation of the ethical command of Jesus.

As man's knowledge increases, change becomes so great as to threaten his identity, because it undermines the very institutions to which the establishment of that identity is related. In the case of religious institutions, change is permitted only with great reluctance. Change which does occur is introduced as clarification or elucidation of "what has always been held."

Today drastic changes in patterns of living and thinking have radically altered the human situation. Yet, given the chance to face a profound religious question bearing upon the purpose of human life, the Church is being pushed (as demonstrated by the pope's encyclical) from an already irrelevant posture into a state of total meaninglessness and hence ineffectuality.

The question is one of ethics: In terms of man's fulfillment of his destiny, is human sexuality separable from procreation? If so, does the separation imply separation from marriage, from heterosexuality, or from deep interpersonal relationship? Or are human sexuality and procreation indissolubly linked? Is procreation not merely a good but an *absolute* good? Is the meaning and purpose of human life simply to exist? Is human existence under any circumstances preferable to never having existed at all? Does the biological differentiation between the respective procreative functions of male and female dictate an inviolable norm for nonprocreative sexual relationships? Must every sexual relationship have a profound interpersonal dimension to it in order to be ethical?

Since theologians within the past decade have begun to ponder issues relating to sexuality which—until Vatican II—had been considered clarified once and for all, it is no longer an ethical question whether or not contraception can be permitted. For revisionist theologians that issue has been settled. It is now clear to them that, in a world threatened by overpopulation, contraception is an ethical imperative.

Against a background of restrictions on contraception, one can resolve current sexual problems only by reexamining the fundamental value at question, namely, reverence for human life. Then it will be necessary to determine an ethical course of action which will adequately protect such a value. Legalistic pronouncements are irrelevant and ineffectual.

We are approaching the time when, unless contraception is more widely practiced, we may lose our reverence for human life. What is worse, we may be *forced* to disregard and even to subvert this fundamental value and thus contribute to the psychic and spiritual confusion which so characterizes our century. This has been brought home most recently by the increased interest in abortion and by the establishment of procedures by which hospitals determine in advance which patients are not to be resuscitated should their hearts stop. In some hospitals this means all those over sixty-five.

Focus on reverence for human life does not mean myopic concern with procreation only. Nor does it mean that there are no other values central to human life which keep personality-damaging licentiousness in check. On the contrary, respect and love of self and neighbor provide signposts for helping the individual judge the line his actions must take if they are to be directed to his highest good.

But attempts to formulate a practical solution of theological issues relevant to sexual acts should not involve a search for "infallible statements" in place of responsible moral decision-making. In other words, while the believer acknowledges that the Spirit will abide with the Church, he should not look for neat linguistic or philosophical declarations. He must trust that God has given him reasoning power as part of Revelation, as a symbol of that in which it participates, part of that in the image of which it is made. Thus man's reason cannot accept finality, for reason is destined to guide him through an evolutionary process in which he is a creative participant.

The preferable alternative to doctrinality in ethics is to view the Church's attempts to teach ethics as a setting out of guidelines. These should produce decisions which ultimately rest in individual conscience and which depend upon the demands of one's identity as defined by relation to God through one's neighbor. Therefore one should not rashly reject all the theological efforts of the past, but, rather, reject the traditional interpretation placed on such efforts. With this in mind, let us consider the application of these principles, first, to the issue of contraception; and ultimately, to all sexual acts. The issue of contraception is the logical starting point because it was against the sinfulness of contraception—as opposed to other acts such as fornication, masturbation, homosexuality, or bestiality—that the contemporary protest against the Church's sexual ethic was initiated.

The 1951 acceptance by Pius XII of the rhythm method of birth control implied that intercourse and procreation were not indissolubly bound together. Science had discovered that nature did not always so link them; man by his inventive ingenuity could capitalize on the discovery.

Implicit in the pope's statement was a rejection of the traditional idea that mankind's procreation was an absolute duty of those who enjoyed marital intercourse, and that any violation of that duty by means of intervention in the biological was a direct offense against God because it contravened the very order of nature. On the contrary, nature can be made subject to reason. Reason therefore liberates man from a so-called "natural law," when that law is unreasonable.

In terms of such freedom and responsibility it is apparent that numerous contraceptive methods cannot be objectively classified as moral or immoral. It is only one's attitude toward their use which can be subject to moral judgment.

Within the framework of each couple's private needs and the community's public needs, the couple must make a free and responsible decision as to the manner in which their sexuality will be oriented toward or away from procreation. As mentioned earlier, however, they are not left wholly to their own searchings. The Church's guidelines are clear. What is more important, the guidelines illuminate the fundamental values of responsible parenthood which are to be respected.

Thus it is neither the minutest prescription of conduct derived from the guidelines, nor the guidelines themselves, which are normative; rather, it is the fundamental values. Parenthood alone does not deserve the exaltation which it has too often been given. It is only responsible parenthood that can claim such a crown. Virtually anyone, married or not, can procreate; so marriage itself is not normative. Marriage may sacramentalize sexual activity, but only numerous other requisites (psychological, emotional, and so forth) for the proper rearing of a child can make procreative sexual activity ethical.

Such a revisionist reinterpretation of the significance of the Church's teaching is not fanciful. It represents an effort of reason, taking its impetus from the pope's own lead, to reflect on what man believes. The power of such a reinterpretation lies precisely in the very notion of revision or reformation which it suggests. Removed from the frozen state of divinely absolutized "natural law" biology, the subject is always open to new revision by means of reasoned human decision.

An immediate conclusion is that no distinction is to be made between methods of contraception, such as use of the condom or the pill, unless the couple's own interpersonal or individual needs dictate the making of such a distinction.

A second conclusion is that if human sexuality can have a nonprocreative purpose to fulfill, then it is at least questionable that this purpose is fullfilled exclusively in marriage —which would utterly repudiate the tradition's insistence that sexual intercourse outside of marriage is strictly forbidden.

The separation of human sexuality in itself from human sexuality as procreative leaves open the possibility that where it is made nonprocreative—whether in circumstances that are marital or nonmarital, heterosexual or nonheterosexual, inseminative or not—it does not have to be surrounded by the *kinds* of restrictions hitherto placed on it. To put it a different way, if sexual activity can be guaranteed nonprocreative, it is no longer hemmed in by the rules and guidelines previously established out of reverence for the life of the potential child.

This does not mean, of course, that sexual activity has no more significance than a game of chess, for example. Nor does it mean that there are no guidelines whatsoever. But the guidelines must be flexible enough to deal with the various attitudes toward sexuality of diverse individuals and groups. Certainly, sexual activity is different from playing chess because sexuality permeates one's whole being, one's entire personality; moreover, the sexual passion is so profound and strong as to be decidedly different from the passion one might have for chess. Sexual activity is also usually shared with another person who must be taken into consideration. However, guidelines are a far cry from prohibitions based on the concept of the intrinsic immorality of an act.

The guidelines for nonprocreative sexual activity are therefore very definite, and they are concerned with the preservation of the integrity of the human personality. To engage in sexual activity that would be destructive of one's own or another's personality is ethically wrong and dangerous. It may be worth noting at this point, however, that the more seriously dangerous it is, the more it is usually associated with and stems from psychological illness. But the mentally ill are hardly models for responsibility in terms of sin.

There are vastly different kinds of sexual activity. In one case it is psychotic and totally promiscuous. In another case —marriage—it is a commitment to exclusivity, permanent union, and dedication to the establishment of a family unit and, possibly, to the rearing of children. Between two such extremes lie the countless other kinds. Where the line is to be drawn with respect to what is moral and immoral is problematic. There can probably be no hard and fast rule. The middle area is never either black or white, but gray.

The individual, however, is not asked to make a decision apart from any guidelines. He is equipped with the fundamental values of human integrity, personal responsibility, love, and consideration. His love for self and others must lead him to show concern for persons and their feelings. Sometimes the decisions may be difficult; but the guidelines —the values of responsible action and of personal integrity— are there, and these must be protected. Some of the guidelines necessary in an earlier age as a protection for the potential child are gone because in the case of nonprocreative intercourse they are no longer necessary. Granted, with their removal comes more personal responsibility. But there comes as well more freedom for growth in humanity and in love. And this is the very meaning of ethics.

To say that in the past the association of sacredness with sexual intercourse was based on its connection with procreation is true. This, however, does not tell the *whole* story. It tells only of the important fundamental basis for an assertion of its sacredness. Sexual intercourse was tied to life—in the sense that it was tied to reproduction. Hence, it could easily be tied to the one apparently nonrevaluable value: existence itself. Yet, despite the acceptance of the legitimacy of sexual intercourse between the sterile and between persons past the age of childbearing, sexual intercourse was still regarded as sacred. For the intercourse-procreation link engendered a profound attitude of sacredness for the responsibility entrusted to man that his sexual potentiality be used for the fulfillment of what clearly seemed to be its main function. And there was as well a profound concern that exception not be made to this usage, for fear that sex would be used in ways that might produce psychic harm. In other words, deep concern was present that moral decision-making regarding sexuality be responsible lest it be abused.

There was nevertheless great unwillingness to place the responsibility for moral decision-making in the hands of the individual. Strong feeling was evident, for example, in the thought of Sanchez who, as we have seen, feared that giving the individual jurisdiction over the seed would encourage him to seek the pleasure of orgasm as his "sovereign good." And, again, there was grave apprehension that the pleasure of sexuality, so strongly attractive, could lead man into abuses.

Time has not eliminated the pitfall of sexual abuse. Therefore it is erroneous to say that today one may remove restrictions on the use of human sexuality *simply* because intercourse may be rendered nonprocreative. Instead, the reason for justifying the removal of restrictions is that a new maturity among men makes their continued imposition unnecessary. But restrictions about honesty, love, and goodness in the use of sexuality remain; these are, in fact, restrictions put on the use of any of man's faculties. It is extraneous legislation—that is, restrictions rooted in fixed concepts of nature, commitment to conservation of the species, and the fear of the social consequences that might ensue should decision-making about sexuality be left to personal judgment—that can be eliminated as man appropriates for himself better developed and expanded models of good and decent sexual behavior.

In short, the new world view is such that restrictions of the *kind* predicated on the natural law doctrine (that is, predicated not on reason but on a commitment by consensus to a fixed world view) are discarded as being no longer meaningful. With this there is a removal of any notion that sexuality, in order to be licit, must have meaning, love, and emotionality as part of it.

Accompanying the new view is an insistence that it is senseless and inappropriate to attempt to render an objective verdict of intrinsic immorality with respect to certain acts by reason of their form. While such acts may be marginally fulfilling in the estimation of our forbears or of Western man, or even of mankind generally, a consensus of this kind is not a rational basis for imputing intrinsic sinfulness to such acts, because it is a value judgment made independently of rational argument.

To destroy the natural law doctrine, to repudiate it, and therefore to insert reason into the matter of human sexuality, is to strike at the very heart of the issue and to force those who defend the doctrine to mount their defense. The issue is basically one that revolves around the role of reason in the discussion. Those who defend the natural law doctrine may be willing to acknowledge that their position is not reasonable—not, however, in the sense that it is *un*reasonable, but simply that it surpasses mere reason. Whether it is or is not in harmony with mere reason is unimportant. They insist that, with or without reason, tradition speaks to them in favor of the rejection of any "artificial" means of birth control. Their reason may hinge on the fact that the area being dealt with here is fundamentally sacred; it is an area of special privilege because it involves cooperation with God in bringing forth new life, and to cooperate with God in this fashion is the supreme human act. Yet this is the source of the conflict, for, as discussed earlier, in the context of a newer world view man "creates" himself by being able to rationally alter the givenness of "nature." This is what is at issue. Men have brought the sacred into being by reading sacrality into meanings and purposes, determined by broad consensus, which seem to them to be the requirements for maintaining the value of life. Yet man is capable of halting all procreation. And he has this power only because it is within his "nature" to be rational. One might say that man has the power only because nature (God) gave it to him. This is why there is a real religious question at issue.

Natural law—as the term applies to gravity, for example —implies a law which is consistent on the basis of the natural conditions which sustain it. A law is either natural (and hence independent of the influence of reason, except to the extent to which man's reasoning power may permit him to overcome its effects) or it is rational—that is, guided by reason. A natural law needs no articulation, but exists independently and is not subject to institutional manipulation.

Yet reasoning is not really the question here; adherence to the natural law doctrine is essentially more a matter of "faith" in the tradition. However, as discussed previously, it is the revisionists' contention that man must submit to the reasonable even in this area, and not adopt the view that there is here a kind of given, unalterable, natural mode of behavior that comes from God himself. Again, this view carries with it the implication that if reason has been allowed to enter into the rule and to change it in this case, then it can likewise in the future enter into and change the situation which may be accepted as the outcome of present reasoning. Further, to find an exception to an absolute doctrine is to remove its very absoluteness; present revision therefore opens up the possibility of continuing future revisions.

One must abandon the traditional prohibition of nonprocreative forms of sexual indulgence, at least insofar as that prohibition is based upon the idea that sexual acts must be ordered to procreation. If nonprocreative sexual activity is accepted as licit in marriage, then one is necessarily left with the obligation to reconsider all such forms, both inside and outside of marriage.

If those who accept the licit use of contraception in

marriage refuse to accept the possibility of considering the licit use of sexuality outside of marriage, then the question arises: Are they making this decision on the basis of an acceptance of the natural law doctrine, and at the same time finding an exception in the area of contraceptive activity in marriage? Or do they have other reasons for their refusal to accept as licit the use of sexuality outside of marriage? One may repudiate promiscuous sexual indulgence on the grounds that it is undesirable, yet not find it sinful on that account. But one who permits nonprocreative sexual activity to the married cannot logically forbid it to the unmarried on the traditional grounds that a child might be hurt or that it is always ordered to procreation if, in fact, one can guarantee in advance that a particular act cannot possibly be procreative. Thus, if the use of sexuality outside the married state is to be forbidden, it must be forbidden on grounds apart from the natural law doctrine; for to accept the revisionist position on the liceity of contraceptive use in marriage is not merely to find an exception to the natural law doctrine, but to destroy it.

In view of this, it seems unreasonable to maintain that there is a difference between allowing a husband and wife to use the condom and allowing them to have anal intercourse, since neither fulfills the natural law doctrine's requirement of insemination in the vagina. Likewise there is no difference between using the condom and *coitus interruptus* or any of the other so-called sins prohibited under the doctrine, such as masturbation, homosexuality, and bestiality. If human sexuality is made nonprocreative, then it must be judged on its own merits because (to stress what has been said before) to render it nonprocreative is to separate it from the sanctions imposed upon intercourse when it was thought that intercourse would ordinarily be procreative. While it is true that other concerns (for example, for the seed, for social consequences) are apparently manifest in the tradition, these are really rationalizations for deeply felt consensus, not rational arguments. They are rationalizations for archetypal concern with the value of life itself, and they are intended to guard restrictions on the use of sex because those restrictions are felt to be protective of life. Thus it is ultimately the link between sex and procreation that lies behind all rationalizations and that is the heart of natural law theory in general and the natural law doctrine in particular.

Rendering sexual intercourse nonprocreative will mean that the inseminative norm, like some of the earlier norms that passed away, is no longer absolute. Earlier requirements, that intercourse not be undertaken in pregnancy or that it be undertaken only in the prone position, were required because of the insistence on the procreative intention. With revisionism we have the acceptance of an expressly nonprocreative intention. The revisionists see this present in Pope Pius XII's own acceptance of the observance of a woman's sterile period as a legitimate means for the regulation of birth. And all would maintain that we have this in the revisionists' acceptance of the use of the condom as a licit means for the prevention of birth. Thus nonprocreative sexuality must be rejudged.

Although restrictions deemed necessary in an earlier era are removed, sexual activity is not reduced to the minimal level of significance but retains importance even apart from procreation. Sexual activity is tied to one's total development as a human person. It can be a profound emotional experience and is, generally speaking, "other-oriented." One is therefore ordinarily dealing with a human interpersonal relationship. There must therefore be guidelines for the proper use of the sex act, and these must serve to protect the integrity of the person. The actualization in any measure of one's sexual potential is a form of self-expression and communication. It is the symbol and the expression of the individual.

Sexuality can express a wide variety of feelings: love, hate, hostility, anger, joy, non-loneliness, togetherness, and the orientation of one individual towards another. Or it can help the individual to gain a larger identity, to lose his self-isolation. Like any of man's powers, it can be used for good.

One of the greatest injustices connected with sexual ethics, however, arose from the insistence by some that sexual acts were always evil, that they had an evil connotation attached to them. This in turn gave them a negative moral meaning. But sexual acts in themselves have no such evil connotation, nor do they have an intrinsic moral meaning of any character—positive or negative.

This does *not* mean that sexual acts in the concrete are devoid, ordinarily speaking, of either meaning or moral valuation. It is simply that the attempt to regulate sexual behavior on the basis of predetermined moral valuations predicated upon cultural customs or supposed intrinsic valuation is, at the least, wrong in concept and, quite possibly, dangerous in terms of proper sexual development.

Certainly sexual acts can have significant effects, either good or bad, and as a result they are either quite rewarding or quite sinful. But such acts may also be relatively rare, while the larger number of sexual acts having little or no meaning are perhaps often silly but seldom sinful. The mistake in our approach to sexual ethics has been our peculiar insistence that this area of human life was somehow distinct from other areas in that reason could not be our guide here. The sacred aspect of life was allowed to give sexuality (because of its proximity to life) an aspect of taboo. And the taboo was often irrational in its effects.[1]

One further point needs to be made in this regard, lest there be those who protest that the hypocrisy of pretending that sexual acts as such have some intrinsic valuation serves the purpose of encouraging or forcing individuals to seek meaningful sexual activity. All of us are created for love, and are discontented without it. In a race bred to close-binding relationships, few men prefer the marginal satisfactions of casual and meaningless sexual liaisons. But let us see them as they are—meaningless. Let us neither condemn nor praise them. Let us characterize them as only marginally fulfilling; and let us do all in our power to help others move toward something better, not by means of taboo but by means of acceptance. In part, at least, the issue arises from the fact that in the case of sexuality—as in so many other cases —one must not be discouraged from experience, as this often implies the greater danger of seriously abridged personal development. Sexuality is too important an area of personal development for such tactics. One can be warned about stigmas attached to loose living and to unwanted pregnancies; but that is as far as this can legitimately be carried. One can be exhorted to seek meaning in all of life, and to use sex well and profitably as a means of self-expression and communication of one's deepest feelings of love. But one ought not to be told that every naive, shallow, or experimental use of sexuality is sinful by reason of evil intrinsic to sexuality.

The human need for meaning in sexual relationships, as in all interpersonal relationships, can be seen in the case of loneliness. The lonely individual does not assuage his loneliness with one sexual relationship or with a hundred, if all are devoid of meaning. Even in a crowd loneliness persists if there is no one to whom a person can relate with some degree of meaning. But this fact does not render meaningless and unfulfilling relationships sinful. Even those who are, for whatever reasons, habitually seeking empty or possibly promiscuous relationships do not seek them precisely as empty or promiscuous.

People plagued with promiscuity or infidelity may lack psychological stability; they may be shackled by unfulfilled psychological needs. Often they are looking to find the perfect, the substitute for "the lost narcissism of childhood," instead of struggling to improve that which is not and cannot be perfect and which really has no need to be perfect. In this case man's "infinite-finite" conflict is characterized by the vain hope of transforming his finitude into perfection by folding himself into the subjectively perfect person, the ego-ideal, the fulfillment of what he thinks would make him lovable.[2]

But if those who seek casual sexual relationships do not seek them precisely as empty or promiscuous, then it is not fair to pass judgment on them as if they were. This is the weakness of any ethical code which is not comprised of guidelines but rather of absolutes. For absolutes tend to crumble when the attempt is made to test them exhaustively. One can almost always find a case in which the rational mode of action is to reject the absolute.

An example of such an absolute is the rule that would permit sex solely within marriage. Some individuals hold that sex is too powerful an element in human life to allow intercourse outside of marriage. They fear the emotions that might be engendered should this be permitted. They also fear that if an attachment is one-sided in a situation of this kind, a person may be hurt; marriage, on the other hand, because it provides a permanent union, protects the individual against this evil. They thus see marriage as offering social protection, enveloping the vulnerability to which one exposes oneself when one loves another person.

In opposition to this view there are those who feel that the fear of unleashing sexual emotion is essentially a weakness because an individual must be able to deal with his sexual feelings as he must with other feelings unleashed in the course of human life. They further feel that the need to sign on the dotted line, as it were, to go through an official external marriage ceremony, may indicate an element of mistrust in the relationship on the part of at least one of the parties. If this is taken as a slur against the female, there are those who would respond that the male may be more capable of separating the physical aspects of his sexual relationships from his emotional involvement in those relationships. Others counter that if the male can do this more easily, it is because he has been conditioned and, in fact, dehumanized, in order to achieve a certain toughness that allows him to make his way in the world. They therefore see the male's ability to suppress his emotions as a weakness rather than a strength.

Some people, then, insist that sexual relationships outside of marriage cannot work. Others are of the opinion that truly meaningful relationships are not necessarily confined to the married state. Some maintain that the sexual relationship does not have to have meaning if each party is fully aware of the other's attitude. Others express concern about the problem of dehumanization, about treating sex like any other commodity. Some would contend that sex is exactly that—a commodity like any other—thus disagreeing with those who want to attach greater importance to it.

The fear of treating sex like any other commodity is that sexual encounter—which, ordinarily speaking, should be more profound than other encounters—might become a fleeting experience that can damage the personality. Conversely, the grave implications so often attached to sexual encounters often force one or both of the partners into a tense conflict which revolves around alternate and radically different emotions. Torn between socioreligious demands, personal priorities, and other more fundamental commitments (psychological, moral), the individual often finds that sexual experience is stripped of its rich meaning. This is why the sexual encounter so often assumes insurmountable and frightening proportions for the adequately sensitive participant.

What is involved in these considerations is not an alteration of fundamental human values or an attack upon them, but a concern that such values be protected. Simultaneously it is a rejection of any attempt to protect such values with a "fence about the Torah" that is essentially beyond repair. There is instead an insistence that such values will be better protected by a shield of reason.

In discussing values it is necessary to understand the distinction that must be made between expressing an ideal and expressing it with the built-in implication that failure to attain it is somehow wrong. Even the use of the word "ought" can carry with it a negative connotation when used to express an ideal. Sexuality ought to be used to express human love—that is an ideal; but one should not feel guilt for falling short of it. For the ideal does not represent the exclusive acceptable or morally good mode for the use of human sexuality. Until the present era the tradition had attributed to certain sexual acts an inherent, intrinsic morality. Masturbation, for example, was seen by the theological writers discussed earlier as always and everywhere, objectively speaking, intrinsically immoral and, if unrepented, deserving of the eternal torment of hell. While it was acknowledged that certain circumstances might mitigate personal responsibility, the action in itself had an objective moral character, an objective moral valuation of evil. The whole question in the present period is whether or not this *kind* of understanding of the morality of sexual acts is correct. If it is not, then it must be changed.

It is the view of this author that, religiously speaking, there is no moral valuation to be placed upon any sexual act in isolation. Sexual acts, especially those outside of a socially accepted norm, can backfire and can create feelings of guilt whether that guilt be religious or neurotic. But this is the consequence of the mores of a given society, and there are those who can deal with this kind of sexual activity without harmful consequences.

Sexuality can no longer be approached in terms of what the individual cannot do. It must instead be approached in the context of an individual's attempt to build a life that is productive and used as one of the means by which the individual is oriented towards growth in self-awareness and openness to self-development. In other words, sexuality is to be used as is any other area of potential in one's life: for developing greater self-consciousness. Properly used in accordance with its intensity and importance, it should serve as an integrating factor in the mature individual's life. Creative development is possible only in a context of interpersonal

132

relationship. No one can mature in an interpersonal vacuum, apart from feedback and response from another. Thus sexuality functions as an important facet of the person's self-development, and becomes a means whereby the individual reaches out to others, a means whereby his life is given direction, energy, and vitality. It therefore becomes a part of the way in which the individual creates himself, and saves himself and others. This is a constructive, positive view of sexuality.

This perspective accomplishes several things. It removes the burden of guilt concerning actions that, although sexual, are essentially meaningless or petty. Moreover, it allows the individual more rationally and more calmly to approach the problems that he faces in attempting prudently to direct the use of his sexuality in his relationships to others. This view helps him to integrate his sexuality into his whole life, rather than to isolate it as a part which is negative and evil and the source of difficulties. In the notion that there is nothing intrinsically evil in any sexual act, there is a certain openness which makes possible a better life-style. Instead of repressing, fearing, and trying to turn away from a part of his personality, one can integrate it into the mainstream of his whole life.

To talk about sexuality in this way is indeed to speak of it in a broader sense than that in which the tradition has ordinarily spoken of it. Yet this is critically essential, for moralists traditionally have regarded each sexual act in isolation rather than as a part of a whole way of life. They saw a single impure act as capable of condemning an individual to hell. Thus, to reject this past analysis is really to reject the idea that an individual could turn himself totally away from God by reason of an isolated thought of little significance in the context of one's whole life.

The determination of moral responsibility was in a sense much easier for an individual when sexual acts had a definitive negative moral valuation placed upon them. Now he bears the burden of freedom and the responsibility of deciding for himself whether or not certain acts are moral or immoral. But it is only by the assumption of the burden of freedom in this as in all of human life that anyone can ever hope to grow to be something better, something more than he is now.

Sex is personal. Consequently its morality must be subject to the highly personal judgment of the individual. Yet because sexuality—though personal—also reaches out beyond the individual, the common good is often at issue; and society has the right to concern itself with sexuality's public aspects. But is it appropriate that moral pressure in terms of taboo and custom should govern the more important public aspects, such as offspring, marriage, and the encouragement of the establishment and stability of families? Who among us today would subscribe to the idea that any worthwhile purpose is served by doling out jail terms to persons caught in their bedrooms commiting acts like contraception, masturbation, homosexuality, bestiality? Yet laws against such acts as these have existed in the past and, in some cases, can be found among existing statutes. Should society use the law this way in order to demonstrate its abhorrence of deviation from certain norms? Is there no more creative, more effective, and more realistic method of dealing with problems of deviance?

When sexuality was expected to be procreative, theologians ordinarily harmonized their rules with social expectations within the procreation-oriented framework of thought. Anything which might have led to illegitimacy or which threatened family stability was deplored. Sexual morality was strict.

Today the picture has changed, largely because contraceptive coitus and de-emphasis on procreation have raised questions about various absolutist viewpoints. Because of the very absolutism of the past law, however, any rethinking is cataclysmic. The result is a whole new mode of thought inclining toward a more rational approach which—by removing the notion of absolute, intrinsic moral valuation—lays heavy stress upon the element of personal moral judgment.

Thus, for example, it may be necessary for one individual, on account of his personal circumstances—either extrinsic or intrinsic—to adjust to a sexual mode of existence quite different from that of others. Shepherds have customarily sought sexual release with their sheep. Prisoners have traditionally resorted to homosexuality for the same reasons. These circumstances are extrinsic to be sure, but there might be intrinsic circumstances of an insuperable kind which might demand similar adjustment.

A great part of the difficulty has always been with the social pressure to conform. In sexuality, as in other areas of human activity, society seeks conformity. But we are now beginning to see how destructive this demand has been, for the individual who must play a role unsuited to him can only be schizophrenically torn apart by the alienation he must suffer when he represses his true self in order to act out the role society requires of him. The effect is as devastating in the sphere of sex as in any other sphere of human activity. The discovery of the essential or intrinsic amorality of sex denies an intrinsic or extrinsic moral norm of an objective nature. Subject to reason, to an understanding of the consequences of actions, and to a commitment to responsibility; and performed in harmony with the purposes of human life, any sexual act takes its morality—whether it be a moral evaluation of good or evil—from individual circumstances and individual intention.

Because persons have values, their sexual acts have value. Because sexual acts are part of the fabric of life, individuals need guidelines. Any development of a sexual ethic must proceed by way of a guideline or by way of models, just as the development of any ethic; and in devising models one cannot eliminate concern or love from his determination. But one may ask whether sexuality should be concerned with only the greatest moments of human life, or whether sex may sometimes have only the equivalent enjoyment value of a chess game. One may also ask about the hierarchy of models: Can sexuality be reduced to the level of minimal significance? If so, does it then become evil or wrong?

What is crucial regarding sexual relationships, as well as any relationship having genuine potential influence on personality, is how it transforms the individual, what it does to him, and what he does with it. There must, however, be no confusion as to the meaning of positive guidelines and ideals set up in an effort to direct constructively human growth and development. To fall short of the guidelines does not necessarily mean that an individual is damaging himself or that he is orienting himself away from his pursuit of the divine. There is, nevertheless, a negative caution. He must ask if anyone, including himself, is being hurt by what he is doing.

In the case of casual relationships, an individual may profit from his experience in some way. Yet even in relationships of this kind, there will be a greater gain proportionate to the individual's capacity for genuine love.

The model of adolescent masturbation is helpful for an understanding of casual relationships, for these follow the adolescent model and are essentially masturbatory in form. The young person is facing a time of great physical development. He is pressured by the urgency of physiological needs of a specifically sexual nature. He is, if anything, behaving in a "natural" manner, and he is hurting no one. The adolescent model often persists, morally speaking, into adulthood. When it does, it may be due to immaturity. What the moralist must ask himself, however, is whether or not it represents sin.

The problem of masturbation has created a moral dilemma for generations of young Roman Catholics. It deserves careful attention, as does the role of the adolescent model in adult life where it is essentially a recapitulation of the adolescent experience and is possibly the result of a failure to mature psychologically. Adolescent masturbation, especially in excess, is an indication of the youth's struggle to come to grips with feelings of a profoundly psychological nature that are being forced upon him by his sociological, psychological, and physical development. In some adolescents feelings of inferiority and insufficiency, for example, are compensated for by excessive masturbation. This excess, psychologically grounded as it is, has less to do with specifically sexual adjustment than with overall personality adjustment; thus adolescents often need psychological support from mature persons. In the case of the casual, promiscuous relationships of the adult, one can see the adolescent model operating. The individual is seeking to compensate for feelings that he cannot otherwise deal with by engaging in the pleasurable release of sexual intercourse.

In the arena of fundamental sexual orientation, individuals most often choose as a sexual object that which their sexual impulse seeks. Yet the biological and psychological makeup of some persons is such that homosexuality is their mode of sexual relationship and response. The prohibition against homosexuality stemmed from the traditional belief that sex was necessarily and intrinsically procreation-oriented. Persons suffering from this socially unaccepted difficulty should be made to realize that their relationships can be good, especially if love is present. They should be encouraged to seek relationships that are meaningful and constructive, and that can contribute to the development of their personality as loving.

It must not be forgotten that the homosexual is at a distinct disadvantage in a society which condemns and persecutes him. He is deprived of certain social and sexual freedoms granted to his heterosexual equals and is burdened with fears and guilt which his heterosexual peers are not forced to share. It is perhaps because of these fears and guilt feelings that homosexuals allow themselves to be so deprived of their human rights—for example, the right to show affection in public.

One of the cruelest aspects of a majority's attempts to lord it over any minority is not merely the inequity involved in the situation, but the way in which the majority evokes the penalty of ostracism. An individual gets his psychic vitality, his desire to be, from his identification with his group, the community of man. Hence to relegate him to a minority is, in effect, to exclude him from the group. No punishment on earth is crueler than this, for to ostracize him is to doom him to ultimate psychic disintegration. To ostracize him because he is black, because he is a homosexual, because he is a Jew, because he is anything else—especially when what he is cannot be remedied—is to chart that person's doom.

Society has tended to encourage the repression of homosexuality (although there seems to be some ambivalence in the way it treats the male homosexual as opposed to the female homosexual). This is unfortunate. Suppression (a conscious act as distinguished from repression which is at least partly subconscious) makes much more sense, since it allows the individual to be a fully human person, one who can savor, appreciate, and enjoy tender feelings for another person of the same sex.

Repression is also a consequence and reinforcement of the notion of the intrinsic evil of homosexuality. It tends to close off a part of the personality and thereby to damage it. It is an effect of closed-mindedness, another example of society's enforcement of conformity at the terrible price of maimed and maladjusted personalities, rendered so by the stifling of individuality and free expression. It is an effect following upon feelings of guilt engendered by fear of authority. The role-playing which religion and society require of the homosexual is no different from the role-playing they require of all who would be truly free. The individual is compelled to repress his true individual identity and to behave according to socially and religiously sanctioned patterns fashioned by consensus. Thus conformity causes him to rip himself apart in order to lead two lives, as it were.

For those who prefer to see homosexuality as a psychological illness, the rate of recovery is so slight as to call seriously into question the legitimacy of referring at all to an apparent cure. This seems particularly true if "cure" is taken to mean the adoption or attainment of a psychological attitude unaffected and uninfluenced by the individual's prior homosexual actions. To speak of achieving a state of growth and development in which the individual attains a state of psychological integration untouched by his previous experiences is to describe the unreal.

What is really of significant interest is whether or not an adult who has been an overt homosexual can, through any means, attain to a greater or lesser degree a successful adjustment to the predominantly heterosexual society in which he lives and even, in some cases at least, to a heterosexual life-style of his own. What is at issue, then, is individual comfort in life. Such comfort is often precluded however, by the guilt, stemming from their sexual needs, which oppresses individuals. That guilt may be religious, or it may be neurotic. Many are victims of a societal neurosis which has as its symptom guilt brought on by fear of social rejection.

Yet the inadequate description of individuals as heterosexual, homosexual, or bisexual in their orientation provides us with a more important insight. Some persons are not consciously aware of the extent of their sexual adaptability; but they know it subconsciously and fear anything that threatens to burst their sociosexual balloon because they are afraid of possibilities of their own subconsciously imagined behavior. If society were truly tolerant, there would be no pressure of this sort, and the effect might be a realization that the division of persons into heterosexuals, homosexuals, and bisexuals is artificial and arbitrary. The division, in fact, is the result of a former world view that saw the preferences of the *apparent* majority as the norm for what it means to be human. It saw human beings as being limited to what they were "given," as it were. It could thus see deviations as illnesses, perversions, and evils. A new world view, however, makes it clear that each individual is uniquely capable of turning every interpersonal encounter into something new, something creative. We are not forced to limit our encounters to recapitulation either of our own past encounters or of the patterns of the majority. We can instead vivify each encounter with creativity. And that creativity can extend to the use we make of our sexual potential as well. For we are not bound to be classified as creatures limited to a given set of sexual habits hemming us in and assigning us to one sexual category or another, some "acceptable" and some "deviant."

The case of bestiality provides an interesting example. The individual who finds sexual release in bestiality has carried the masturbatory model into the area of animal affection. Feeling the need for communication and affection, he apparently thinks that with an animal he can find the kind of relationship best suited to his needs. Such an individual may have such psychological fears about attempting to get close to another human person that he resorts to animals which he finds more docile and easier to communicate with. Denied such activity, he might never progress beyond wishing for it. Permitted it, he might indeed progress beyond it. But, in any case, where is the harm in it?

Here a word on marriage may be appropriate. Through marriage an individual chooses to create himself in a certain way as a result of having adopted a particular relationship toward another human being. Thus to marry is really to alter one's very being, since one creates himself as a new being by entering into the marital relationship. Marriage is thus an existential way of life.

To alter one's life-style by creating oneself as a married individual is likewise to adopt an orientation of one's life toward parenthood. Or rather, one can adopt this special additional orientation toward parenthood; if one does, then the marriage needs even greater stability, for oriented now toward parenthood, it extends itself to still another person— the child.

There is in the case of marriage a harmful situation

analogous to the rigid treatment given sexuality. Marriage is treated as an absolutized kind of relationship, the details of the "ideal" marriage being spun largely out of notions about what society has thought best for the proper rearing of offspring. However, in an age like the present one, an age of tremendously rapid change in attitudes toward the social structure and environment, the weakness of the static, absolutized conception of any kind of interpersonal relationship is made especially clear. For ours is an age which is witnessing a breakdown of the fundamental values of a social system which fights to remain unchanged despite realistic priorities which cannot be met without change. Moreover, the rapidity of technological achievement tends only to heighten the frustrations of those seeking social reform and thus further militates against a philosophy of commitment to institutions.

Motives for marriage have traditionally been seen as representing a broad spectrum of possibilities; but mythology about marriage has tended to focus on romantic concepts of eternal monogamous fidelity in a union in which love grows stronger with each day. In this model, sexuality plays the critical role of symbolizing that union and, to some extent at least, of cementing and sustaining it.

But marriage is many things to many people. To most it seems a way of life into which they found their way largely as a result of social pressure, custom, and the expectancy of their families—not to mention the fact that cultures have made marriage the only really acceptable route for a free, respectable, and welcome enjoyment of a public sexual relationship. Yet it is regrettable that people feel forced to marry in order to have sex. The satisfaction of sexual needs ought not to be attainable exclusively through marriage, because marriage is a way of life oriented toward goals far superior to anything so petty and so trivial as the social or religious *legitimation* of sex.

However misguided some persons may be in getting married, most realize sooner or later that an interpersonal relationship in which so much depends upon sharing requires great personal consideration of and accommodation to the partner. Where this is not achieved, the relationship is no longer viable; and regardless of the various benefits derived from the marriage, an end to it will follow for those who are not prohibited by considerations of an economic, religious, or charitable nature.

Marriage does not make sex tolerable. But sex does give marriage a special character because it forges a unique physical and psychic bond between two persons. Marriage is possibly not susceptible of definition. In marriage two unique individuals choose to establish some kind of relationship in which they share their lives and destinies to a greater or lesser extent. As institutionalized by Church and state, the relationship is intended to last until one partner dies; it is the basic unit of the social structure and is taken as the normal environment for the procreation and rearing of the young. Numerous cultural and other accretions surround it, and these vary from one society to another. The character of the relationship and the extent of the sharing vary markedly, depending upon the personality composition of each of the individuals.

What defines marriage is its exclusivity, but the rich rewards of exclusivity come at a cost. The considerable benefits which can come only from the lifelong interpersonal commitment of marriage are acquired only at the expense of a great deal of work exerted for the sake of making the marriage successful. Couples who enter marriage blindly run the grave risk of failure unless they quickly realize that they must work hard at the marriage if it is to return the dividends they hope for. Marriage means making oneself terribly vulnerable for the sake of the tremendous love and joy that mutual vulnerability can bring. Indeed, a desire to love fully and deeply is perhaps the only force strong enough to release the innermost wells of love from the defense mechanisms with which such sensitivities are shackled. Only great love can insure that such vulnerability is not exploited through the abuse of sexual intimacy. Only such vulnerability, however, can permit marriage to foster a friendship in which each partner matures in a joint process of creative development. But that vulnerability needs the shield of great love.

Love is giving. When it is present, the lover is motivated more deeply by the desire to give than to take. On this deeper level sexuality attains a significance which it does not have in and of itself when considered as merely another function like excreting or eating. For sexuality, placed at the service of love, is transformed. More a desire to please the beloved than to appropriate personal pleasure, it becomes a means of committing oneself to the fulfillment of another. Again, this is not to deny the less profound uses of the sexual potential. It is, however, to affirm the profounder uses of human sexuality as a means of the expression of human love. Sex without love may be without interpersonal meaning (this is not to say that it is without value); but if sex is honest, it cannot be intrinsically sinful.

One point, however, should be kept clearly in mind. The fact that sexual acts are in themselves amoral does not by any means imply that they are in all ways as morally significant as other morally neutral actions, such as playing a game of chess. For sexual acts carry with them a far greater potential moral significance, even if that significance is really more the result of social and cultural conditioning than of the power of sexual passion.

The reason for this lies in the fact, already pointed out, that sexual acts are—in some societies, at least—a means of self-expression and communication. And even when such communication and self-expression are only symbolic, there can be at issue a question of human relationship. And such human relationship is the very stuff of life itself, for the individual is constituted by his relationships. Establishing a human relationship is an extremely delicate matter. To

**143**

relate is to go out of oneself, to seek the other, to run the risk of disappointment and even hurt. But the mere fact of risk should not deter attempts to relate.

The close connection possible between sexual acts and human relationships, however, requires watchfulness to insure that the acts, like all other means of interpersonal communication, be used responsibly in obedience to the lordship of Jesus. There is always the danger in human relationships of using others instead of loving them, but this is the basic freedom of human life. The opportunity to love must be embraced, not eluded. Nevertheless, sexuality must not be *forced* to carry emotional baggage which it does not always necessarily bear. Who is to say that sexuality for some persons in some societies cannot always perform its many functions in isolation, so that reproductive sex is one thing, sex for excitement is another—all without harm— simply by reason of the conditioning process of a social structure and culture different from that of the English-speaking world?

A rule of ethics, then, is rather simply established from a consideration of what it is to be human. To be human is to reach out in an effort to relate to others through love. Hence an individual's ethical obligation arises when another is reaching out toward him, when another is making himself vulnerable by reaching out; he must insure that he does not take advantage of the other's vulnerability to be hurt. What is asked of him, ethically speaking, is that he behave toward the other as he—in the same circumstances—would wish the other to behave toward him.

One means of setting out moral guidelines is to offer models of human behavior after which a person can pattern and pass judgment on his own actions. To do this is essentially to set out a hierarchy of kinds of human actions. While the central action remains fundamentally the same, the circumstances and conditions surrounding it usually place it in one of several categories of activity. It then becomes possible to judge these activities on the basis of the role that a given model fulfills in human life with respect to the development of the human personality. In the case of sexuality, one then considers the various kinds of sexual acts in relationship to the extent to which love or concern is present or absent and on the basis of whether the presence or absence of this love or concern causes injury to oneself or one's neighbor or is essentially noninjurious.

The problem of defining sexuality is a difficult one. Even a biological definition is, if not really impossible, at least problematic. Biologically speaking, sexuality refers to a physical attribute of the person, that is, maleness or femaleness. Or sexuality can mean a physical form of intercourse between persons carried out under certain biological laws. It must, however, be analyzed as not only an attribute of the person but of his personality as well. Sexuality is therefore more than a physical biological act; it is a form of communication and of self-expression.

Sexuality can be seen as a wish to be immortal. Or, taken from the viewpoint of sexual complimentariness, it represents the possibility of creating a unique reality, a union of two persons.

As a form of communication and the self-expression of an individual, in particular as a means whereby the individual expresses his deepest feelings, sexuality can convey the need that an individual feels for affection, for release, for pleasure, for love. For some individuals sexuality represents the peak of ecstasy. Like peyote, betel, or alcohol, sexual experience is used by some to seek a larger identity or a completeness, a loss of the individual's aloneness and isolation, and a particular unification with ostensibly psycho-spiritual facets of existence. Seen in isolation as merely a discrete act, the fulfilling of a biological operation of the human body, the sexual act is one which releases tension and provides pleasure. When yoked to love, sexuality is concerned with the transformation from Eros, a selfish love, to Agape, an unselfish, giving love. With love, it is tied to the willing of the good of another person. Tied to abuses, it has the evil possibilities of so many of the other acts of human life. It can be used as a means of aggression, domination, or status-seeking.

Because man is freed by his intellect from the mechanical demands of the natural, he alone among the creatures of this earth can deliberately choose to use the numerous possibilities for variety in his sexual expression in order to give expression to himself. Thus each mode of sexual activity is a different form of self-expression. There is no canonized mode. There is, however, a range of productivity in the various modes of sexual self-expression. There is likewise a range of social acceptability, a range of social and psychological comfort.

As previously mentioned, the individual who expresses himself sexually in a mode that is socially unacceptable may suffer religious guilt if this form of sexual expression is prohibited by his religion, or neurotic guilt if he cares a great deal about what others in his society think of him. If, however, he is able truly to internalize the principle that any mode of sexual self-expression is in itself indifferent and that its ethical, psychological, and growth-value depends not upon the form it takes but rather upon its substance, then he is on the way toward freeing himself from any kind of guilt feelings. The substance of his act of sexual self-expression is independent of its external form, structure, or mode; it depends instead upon the way in which it fits into the pattern of his relationship to the principal constituent elements of his life.

Now is the appropriate time for the adoption of new attitudes toward acts prohibited in the past, such as contraception, fornication, masturbation, homosexuality, and bestiality. A genuine innovation in sexual ethics is possible. But such an innovation implies a new creation. And the creation of a new sexual ethic can only follow upon the existence of a new attitude. That new attitude does exist. It is part of a new world view, itself the effect of man's achievement of a new consciousness. And because that

146

new consciousness transcends the old, and that new world view transcends the old, so too that new creation of a sexual ethic transcends the old.

What is new, therefore, is an attitude which of necessity rejects the past approach to sexual ethics, with its blanket prohibition of acts as intrinsically evil and always gravely serious if they do not conform to a specific concept of "nature."

It may be objected that besides tradition there is a scriptural basis for prohibiting acts such as fornication, homosexuality, masturbation, bestiality, contraceptive intercourse, and the like. Yet all would agree that Christian morality is almost entirely the morality of the Old Testament, especially as it concerns Christian attitudes toward sexuality. And advances in scriptural scholarship make it clear that moral pronouncements found in Scripture are simply the expressions of the author's convictions as to how everyday problems of living must be resolved in accordance with the thrust of the Judaic-Christian ethical message. They cannot be assigned in themselves—as isolated pronouncements—the absolute value of inerrancy. This value is attributable only to the total scriptural narration of the crucial necessity of faith as man's response to God's revelation, on the basis of which he is alone saved from all that threatens him with loss of meaning and intelligibility. In short, values being protected at a particular period may lose their validity in another time and place.

One clear result of the investigation thus far is that sexual behavior follows many possible models. As used here, however, "model" does not mean an external, but an internal, psychological form. There is a special model for sexual behavior in connection with human love. Sexuality can be used as a unique, highly passionate physical symbol of union between two persons who love each other. But it does not thereby possess a special greatness or sacredness in itself. Sexuality attains unique value if, and only if, the symbol has meaning, that is, if there is a reality behind the symbol of one individual really caring for another as he does for his own flesh, for his own body, and for his own spirit.

The particular model of sexuality tied to human love can indeed serve as an ideal model for human beings—but only with certain reservations. It is simplistic to say that one ought to utilize sexuality for the purpose of expressing love. To couch this ideal in such language—in particular, to use the word "ought"—can prove to be more of a stumbling block to healthy growth and development than a stepping-stone to psychic integrity. The language itself can get in the way of proper communication and make what is said seem stronger than was intended. Such language can create guilt in one who uses sexuality in a fashion other than the ideal. This is dangerous and wrong. Those who would set out moral guidelines, ideals of human behavior, must carefully spell out the distinctions between that which is required and that which is desired. The moralist must never sacrifice his own moral integrity to what he may think is expedient, not even to what seems to be expedient for the common good.

In all of man's life there are paradoxes. For the man who is approaching the mystery of God through moral or ethical considerations, a clear paradox arises with respect to the problem of good and evil. What the paradox teaches us, however, is extremely valuable; for, as it helps us to understand ourselves—that is, to reach greater self-consciousness—it tells us much about the mystery of God.

The key element in the evolution of man as man is, of course, his reason. At each step in his development man's reason has won for him greater power, greater wisdom, and thus greater potential. As is the case with every achievement of reason, each step forward brings with it not only the possibility for greater humanization, but the possibility for greater dehumanization as well. Man's ability to split the atom, for example, has given him tremendous power for good; but it has also put into his hands a tremendous potentiality for evil. At each stage of his development man creates what is essentially indifferent in itself or what ordinarily possesses some basic value. But what determines the moral value of any achievement of man is not its intrinisic value but rather what man does with it. The same is true of moral actions.

There has been a tendency to put positive or negative valuation upon actions which have no such valuation intrinsic to them; but, as with all of that which man can do, they must be given valuation by reason. In the past, societies have generally tended to absolutize the valuation, whether positive or negative, which they placed on certain acts. In so doing they failed to appreciate the fact that such valuations are, at best, only relative.

Human life takes its meaning from the development of human potential. The fulfillment of an individual is progressive; it depends upon the expansion of the person, upon his growth to self-consciousness. Satisfaction comes from fulfillment of purpose, individual growth, the joy of knowing more. But even this development is meaningless if it does not pervade all the areas of individual personal experience. All experience, all knowledge, is empty if it finds no application in the fact of living. Thus the individual's completeness demands that the thrust of his life, especially in the areas of his struggle for survival and of his relationship to his fellow-man, be integrated. His life then must provide personal present satisfaction. If such satisfaction is too long deferred, there is danger that serious dissatisfaction might threaten the repression of his very humanity. The key to this kind of integration of the individual is found in his life-style. If it is autonomous and selfish in nature, then the individual lacks outer-directed commitment. Love thus plays the critical role in growth to self-consciousness and is in fact the greatest single integrating factor in human life, growth, and the development to psychic integrity.

Sexual expression therefore has greater meaning in proportion to its use as a means of communicating one individual's absorption with another, that is, love. When an individual establishes rapport with and respect for another, when he finds such goodness and attractiveness in another that he becomes other-directed to the point of being concerned for the happiness, persistence in being, and fellowship of another, then he loves the other. He wants to benefit from and to possess the other; but he will want even more to please, to serve, and to provide for and even die for the other. He may likewise find expression of any or all of these feelings in the demonstration of his emotional attitudes toward the beloved; and sexual communion in varying degrees can provide a distinctively intense and highly symbolic means of expression and communication of his love, particularly because of the way in which sexual acts serve as a means of providing pleasure to the beloved.

Sexuality is paradoxical. It represents not merely a problem but a manifestation of the general mystery of what the "divine" is. The myth of the bisexual divided into male and female teaches us the lesson of man's isolation. Man is alone and feels this aloneness. He yearns for togetherness with his fellows. Yet he faces his own inner conflict over his desire to be autonomous and his concern for and need for others. Sexual union can bridge the gap among men, although it does so only momentarily. The individual's isolation, his selfishness, and his autonomy are broken only by his passion, his emotion. While longing for togetherness, he fears it as well. For he sees it as having the power to rule him, to force him to do what careful reflection might counsel against. He often lives in a society which places proportionately meager value upon the sheer joy of sharing or giving and is thus inclined toward suspicion of just such a process.

But there is likewise a paradox of life. The transience of this life can dramatically put things into perspective, can actually help us to make the absurdity of the transience less tragic. This is part of the mystery.

Time grinds a sharp axe. Those bright and painful

moments of time-consciousness which we all experience add a dimension of existential crisis to our lives, and the strongest demand of that dimension is honesty. Often, in fact, time-consciousness gives an individual a clear indication that he has indeed been living falsely, wastefully, inauthentically —as though he were immortal. This raises a religious question, since some men solve the problem of the givenness of death in an inauthentic fashion which they nevertheless label religious, instead of solving it in a truly religious fashion. They substitute a "proven" and secure knowledge of beyond-the-grave immortality for the believer's hope, which springs from genuine suprarational faith in Jesus. Many are merely pulling the wool over their own eyes, operating under the smug principle of reward, or living under the calculating "wager" concept. What is critical is that one should not be fooled into forgetting that this life, at least as presently understood, ends in death and is characterized thereby; even those who hope for immortality ought not to allow that fact to alter the present task of living authentically this life which ends in death. It has been a dangerous teaching indeed which has dismissed the meaning of death for our present life by reminding us of life after death. For, as Saint Paul tells us, we know little of that life.

It has not been a mistake to tie sexuality to love but rather to tie it exclusively to romantic love. The individual's nature as a sexual being is not at all limited to procreative sexual activity, to romantic sexual activity, to passionate sexual activity. A human being is simply a sexed person, and sexuality has the possibility of playing a role in his every act of love. It has a part in his love of God and his love of neighbor. If it is true that each individual finds God only in his neighbor and loves God only in his neighbor, then it is likewise true that in every act of love of God on the part of man a sexed human being is loving another sexed human being. What is important is that man learn to love, that he be so concerned with loving his fellowman that he transcend the imposed fears and taboos of an ignorant society or culture.

A thoughtful examination of the tradition and a careful rethinking of the ethics of human sexuality yield the immediate conclusion that moralists were in error in trying to assign to sexual acts an objective intrinsic moral valuation. It made for interesting reading perhaps. It simplified moral problems in a sense. Although it may have seemed on the surface that leading a good, moral, Christian life was difficult because all directly venereal use of sexuality outside of marriage was sinful, there was nevertheless a certain kind of moral simplicity about this kind of view, since it provided an absolutely clear set of rules.

With the rejection of an intrinsic moral valuation of sexual acts, a number of difficulties arise. Sexual morality is not so easily derivable. It clearly cannot be codified. One is forced to assume the burden of personal responsibility with respect to his use of his sexual potential. Responsibility, however, is the property of the adult person. It is, after all, only the child who needs to see morality exclusively in terms of black and white. An increased responsibility has its own rewards. Most particularly, the responsible mature individual possesses the freedom to deal creatively with human situations. The one hemmed in by a code ethic does not possess such freedom.

With objective intrinsic moral valuation removed from sexual acts in the abstract, there are interesting ramifications for the sexual ethic in particular, and for ethics in general. In particular, there is a theological movement away from an absolutized doctrine set down in terms of a code of action with which each isolated act must be in harmony. Such a movement is in the direction of greater personal freedom, and towards an appreciation of the burden and risk assumed by the individual as the price of his progress as man. When one begins to use his reason, his greatest gift, then he is truly acting as man. However, by being more self-consciously aware of what God intended him to be, by growing in his humanity, and by acting out his own evolution in an ever more self-directed fashion, he grows away from infantile *ir*religious dependence upon God toward a profounder but undeniably riskier faith-dependence upon the God-orientation of his own evolution. For he himself must now bear the burden of so orienting that evolution. He thus frees himself from the shackles of the "natural" where sexual acts are concerned; but the new freedom carries with it the burden of responsibility for the decisions he makes.

Another effect of the reevaluation is a realization of how dangerously inhuman it is to attempt to make objective value judgments about actions independent of persons, situations, and the weighing in the balance of other human values and goals to which sexual acts, like any human acts, can be a means. While it is, of course, wrong to think of using an intrinsically evil means to any end—however good —it is likewise wrong to label evil that which at worst may be merely less than ideal, different from the norm, immature, or even in some cases somewhat degrading. Clearly, in an age in which human ingenuity can adequately provide for the removal of certain social, economic, and medical evils attached to the broader use of man's sexual potential, where —except in the minds of those constrained by taboos and other queer notions—is the harm in an expanding set of models for the use and enjoyment of human sexuality?

A further effect of much of this reevaluation is the realization that efforts to discern the good, to characterize the ethical person, and to measure the quality of Christian responsibility are as vast as man himself. Even the ethic of the situationist has its limitations; for personal considerations of freedom, growth, and relationship make possible different Christian responses on the part of different persons even in identical circumstances. Moreover, the variety of personal responses to Christ's lordship makes possible even radically different options on the part of a given person in a given set of circumstances. This is why it is

**153**

impossible for any code, however broad, to be more than an attempt at setting out guidelines, just as belief-statements can be no more than human efforts to articulate the experience of faith as it is known by individuals singly or collectively. Any attempt to absolutize a moral code is surely as fraught with dangerous shortcomings as is the attempt to absolutize a theology of belief-statements. The first leads to blindness in defense of moral security against moral risk; the second leads to blindness in defense of "orthodoxy" against "heresy."

The attempt to codify an intrinsic objective morality of sexual acts is another example of the self-righteousness which stands as the very antithesis of true Christian morality. Christ's standard of ethical righteousness and love of neighbor teaches what men—especially when they are in the majority—find most difficult: tolerance. Indeed, where sexuality is concerned—as in so many areas of human life—tolerance and vision are perhaps at once the most uniquely Christian, the most self-fulfilling, and the most important aids to authentic spiritual discovery.

## Footnotes 5

1. One is reminded here of Hans Küng's concern that "the sixth commandment was inordinately overrated." Küng, in his *Truthfulness: The Future of the Church* (New York: Sheed & Ward, 1968), notes: "According to the manuals of moral theology in the post-Tridentine period—one could find very striking examples even today—all sins against the sixth commandment are mortal sins." Küng makes reference to Bernard Häring's *The Law of Christ* (Westminster, Md.: The Newman Press, 1966), in which he writes that "there is no slightness of matter (*parvitas materiae*) in any fully deliberate indulgence of sexual gratification." It is Häring's view that "the objection that the rigor of this teaching concedes to the sixth commandment an unwarranted priority even over the great commandment of love can certainly not be sustained."

2. Freud described this "ego-ideal" as that part of the superego which contains images and attributes that the ego strives to acquire in order to maintain narcissistic equilibrium.

# EPILOGUE

This book raises some questions to which others might wish to address themselves. To reject the extremism of theologians who preoccupied themselves with concern for the seed of life is legitimate, for their view created a monstrous absolutism that eventually crumbled of its own weight. But to reject that absolutism does not tell the whole story. The theologians were concerned that allowing one exception might lead to another and another, until finally the whole thrust of Scripture and tradition would be destroyed. The thrust of the tradition—in which all sexual sins were seen as objectively grave—is destroyed by virtue of the fact that the absolutism of the prohibition is destroyed. Despite this, however, at least part of the thrust of Scripture and tradition can remain.

In fact, if one sees the Church as a community, one can hardly take arbitrary positions in theological matters independent of the structure, leadership, and common experience of that community. On the contrary, serious questions have been raised in this book about innovation in sexual ethics and the structure, function, and authority of the Church as a historical community with a legacy of Scripture and tradition. Surely, the ecclesiological issues raised in that context are important. Yet for the believer who is open to a psychic world-orientation predicated upon an understanding of man as rational and free, and involved creatively in his own evolutionary process of becoming, these issues cease to be problematic. For his theological discourse is then carried out in a context in which the normative roles of Scripture, tradition, and authority partake less of static doctrinality than of evolutionary pattern. And one who would propose to theologize within such a context must then run the risk of speaking to those who are not ready to hear him. His final judge can only be the history of the Church when time has finally passed out of existence.

In all of recorded history, ethics has been understood in relation to society and culture. One of the greatest questions has always concerned the matter of whether or not any given action is always and everywhere wrong. If immorality can be reduced to that which harms one's self or others, are some acts always wrong? It seems possible that this is so, that some are always destructive, antisocial, or at the very least outside of the realm of those things which society values highly for its purposes (especially survival). However, to associate some of those acts with mortal sins, with hell, is too primitive and unwarranted. Let it be clear that it is unacceptable to prohibit as absolutely and intrinsically evil that which a given society does not like or which it finds to be counterproductive to what it devises as its own static and unchanging design for attempting to deal with the unintelligibility and mystery of life—an area of deep human need into which it is so easy to introduce sexuality because of its association with procreation and hence with the one nonrevaluable value: existence itself. It is wrong for society as a whole, or for any person or group of persons, to assign an absolute value of divinity to any act in an effort to gain sanction for the repudiation of acts which are deemed unsuitable for the maintenance of a given social structure or even of the species itself, however noble these goals may appear. The ends, however desirable, do not justify illicit means.

As indicated in Chapter 1, an ethic cannot be really understood apart from an attitude concerning whether or not there exists any meaning—ultimate or finite—in human life. Reason is indeed the "law" of man's nature, but like many laws it is not enough. Reason is in fact its own worst enemy. For there is another "law" in man—feeling. And reason is often defeated by emotion. Questions of life and death significance may depend far more on an individual's psychic state than upon the depth of his ability to reason. When reason has spoken and driven man to question even reason itself, there still remains in man a thirst that demands to be slaked. No one should ever underestimate that thirst, for it is infinite. In each man it is a burning thirst for life and love. And he who knows that thirst knows, by desire at least, the divine. For the divine is revealed to man in terms of his need. Reason is not enough by which to live life, but it is a beginning. It is an infallible guide for judging the inherent rationality of all options, although it stands in need of supplementation. But to yield to unreason in an effort to supplement reason is totally unacceptable, however convenient or even comfortable.

Risk, suffering, faith—and, above all, love—these are more worthy of man.

1850